I0693889

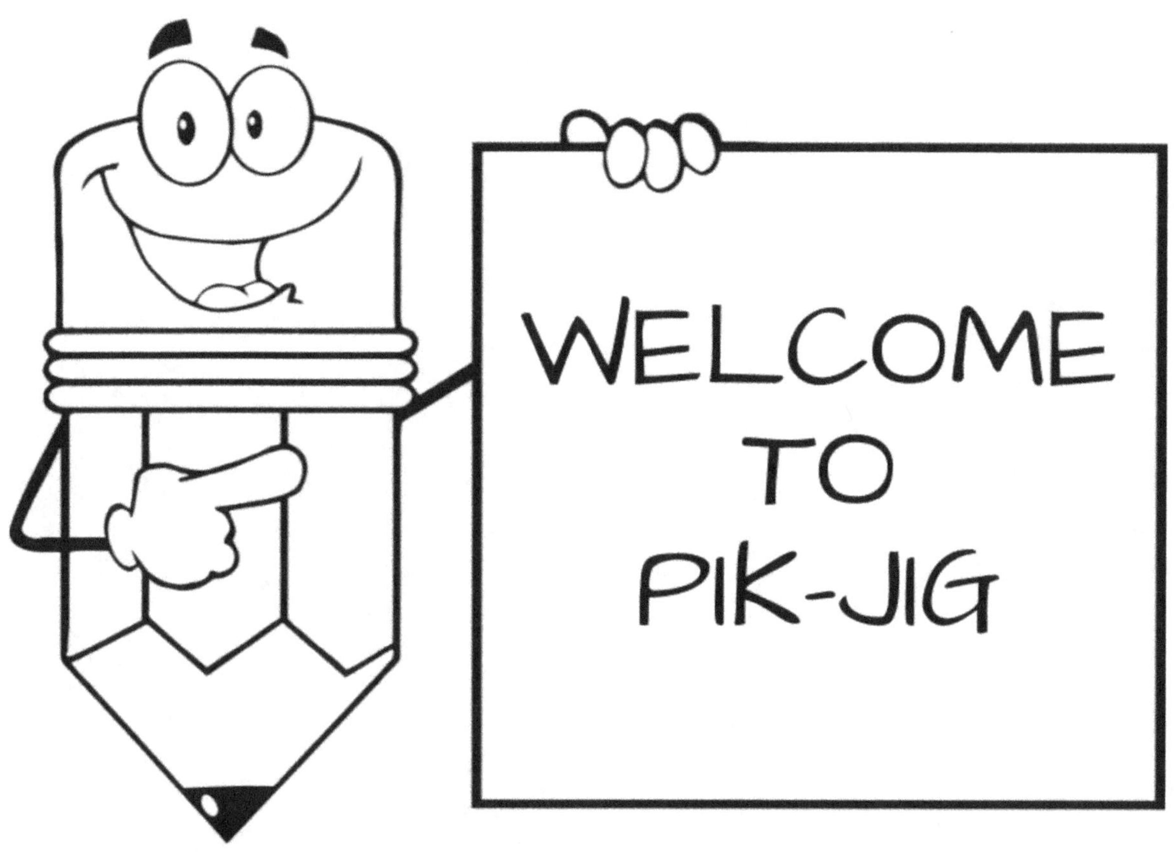
WELCOME
TO
PIK-JIG

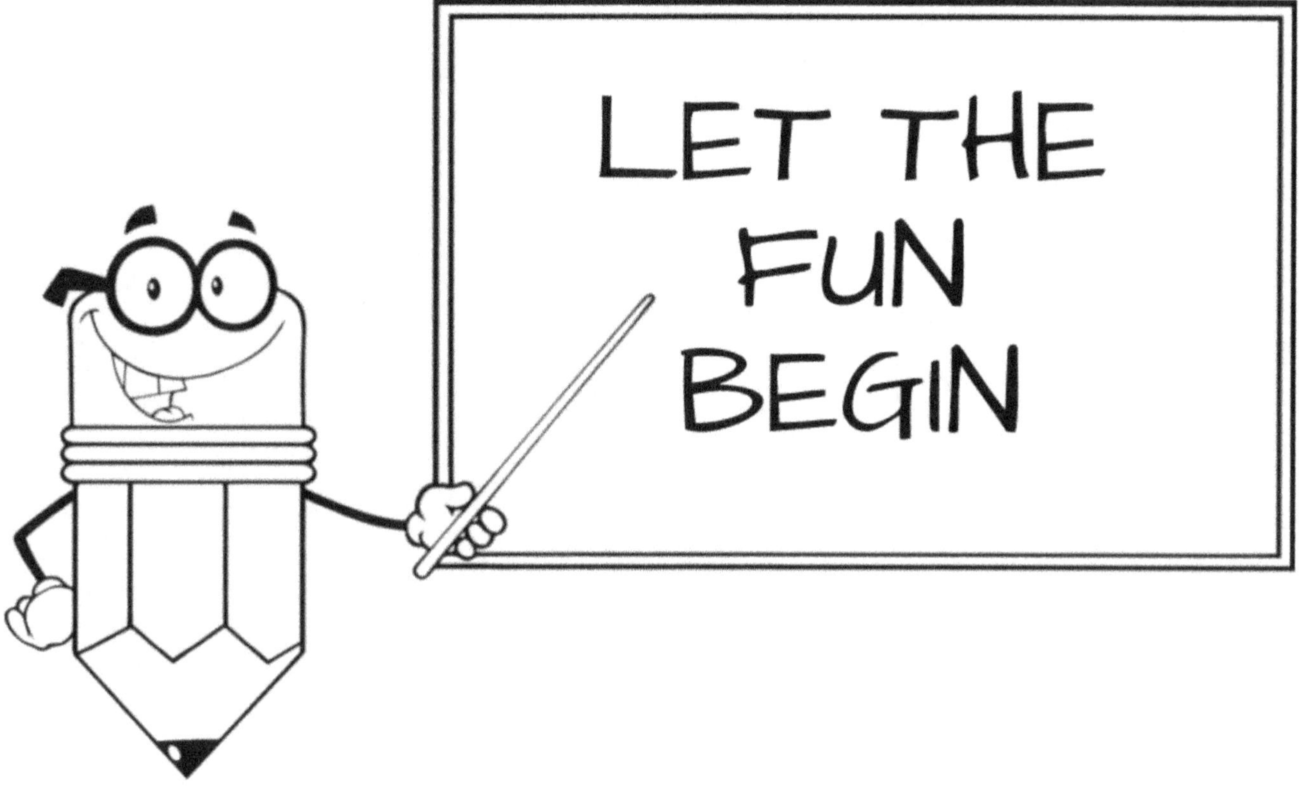

LET THE
FUN
BEGIN

INSTRUCTIONS

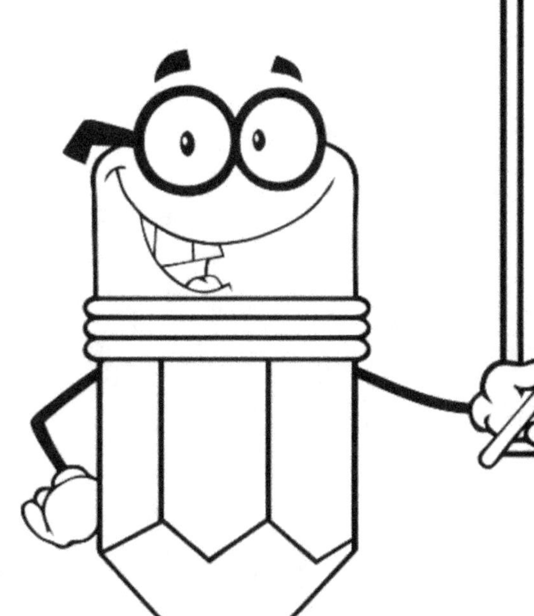

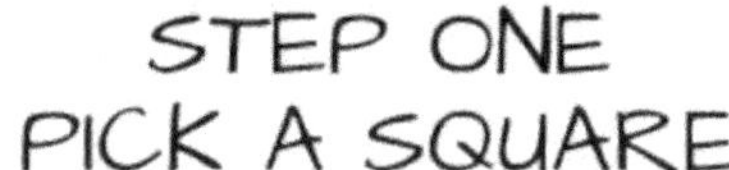

STEP ONE
PICK A SQUARE

STEP TWO
FIND THE SQUARE ON THE GRID BY
MATCHING THE COORDINATES

STEP THREE
DRAW WHAT YOU SEE AND WATCH
THE MAGIC UNFOLD

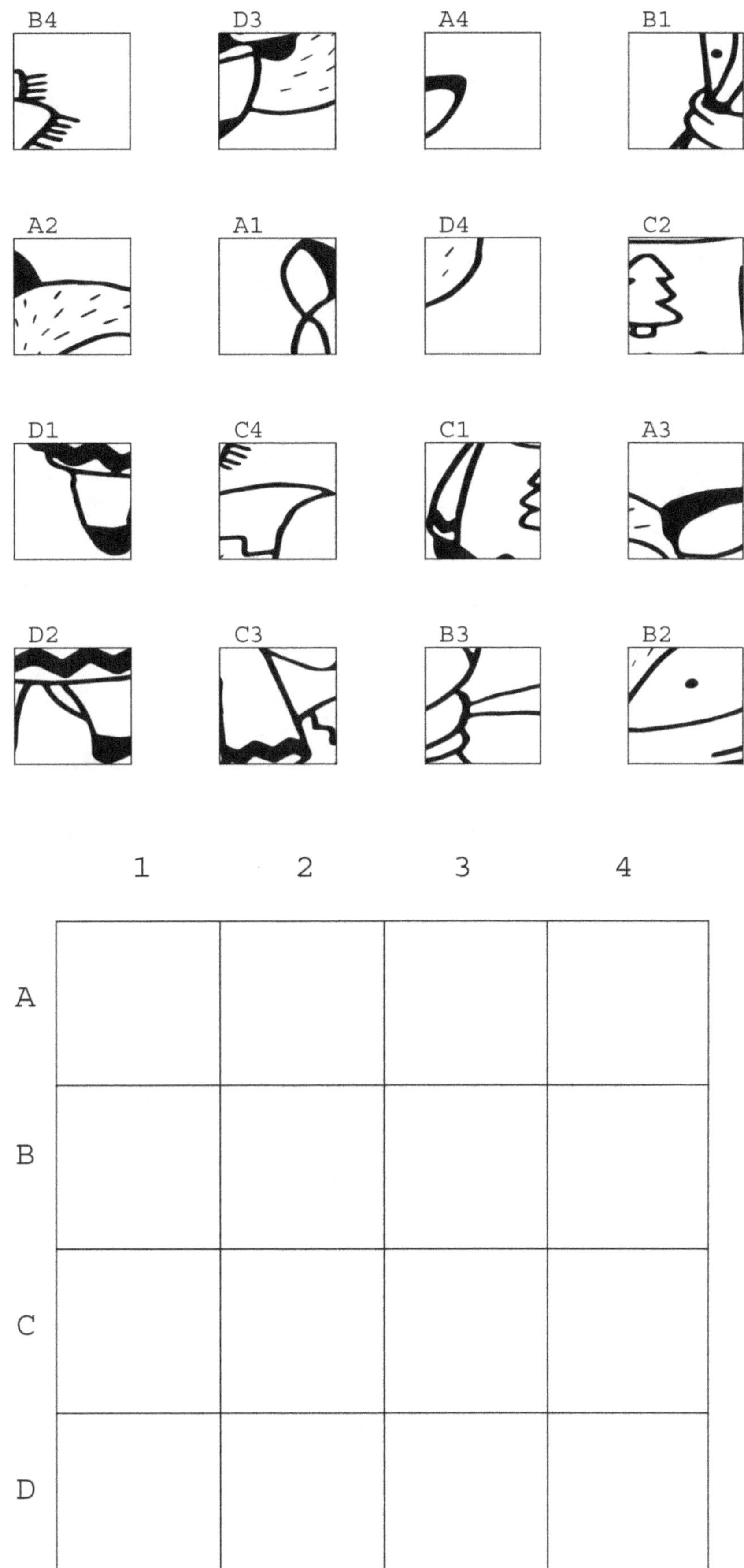

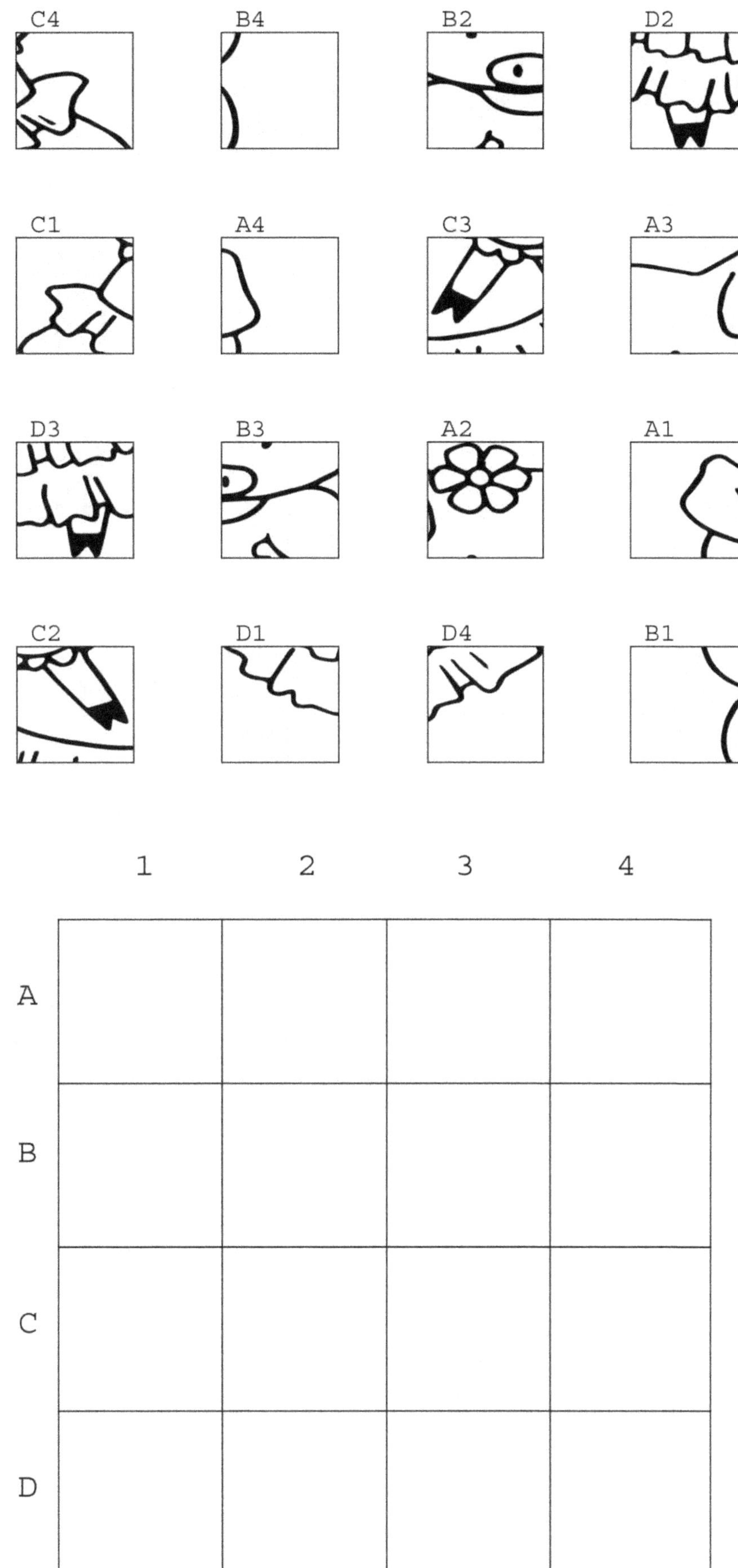

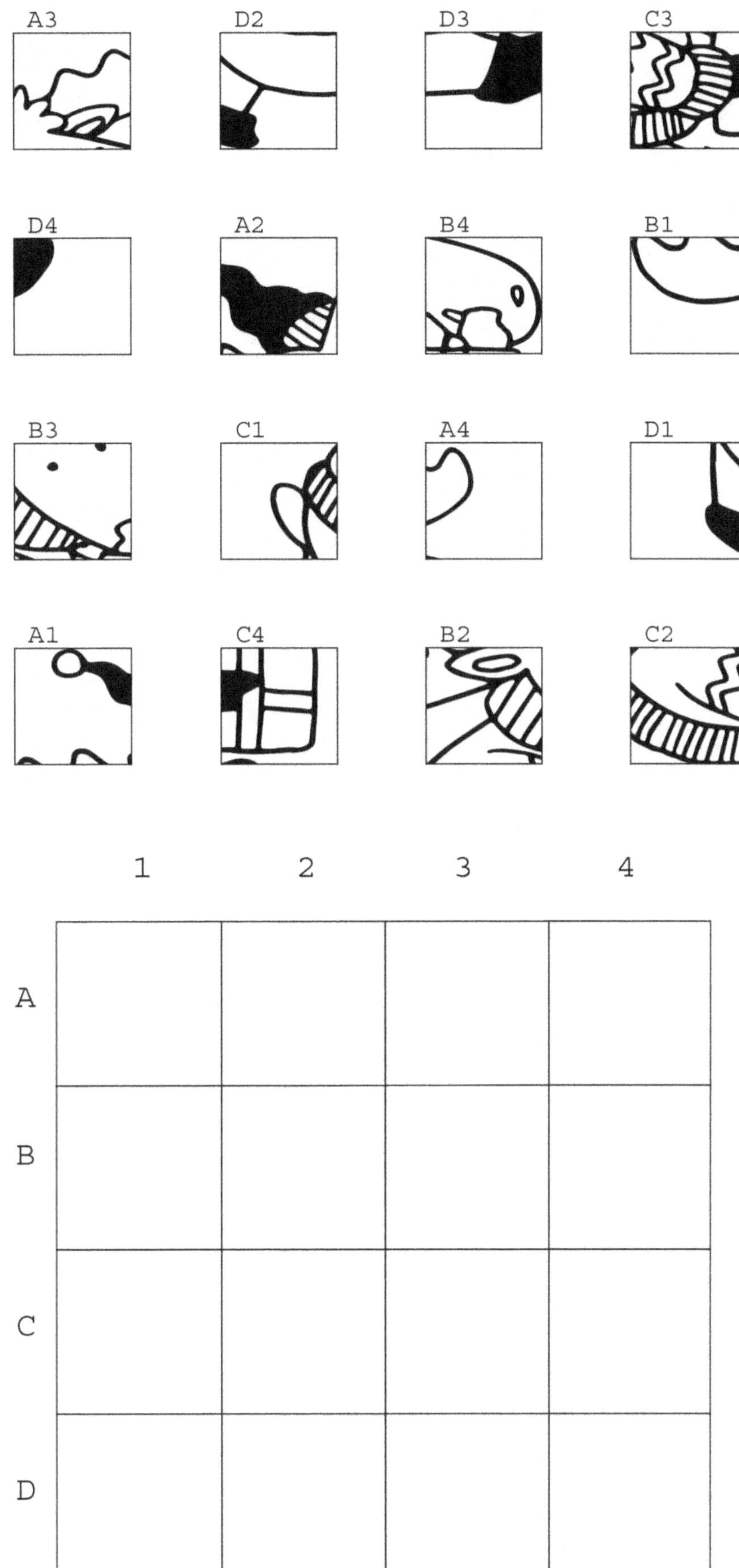

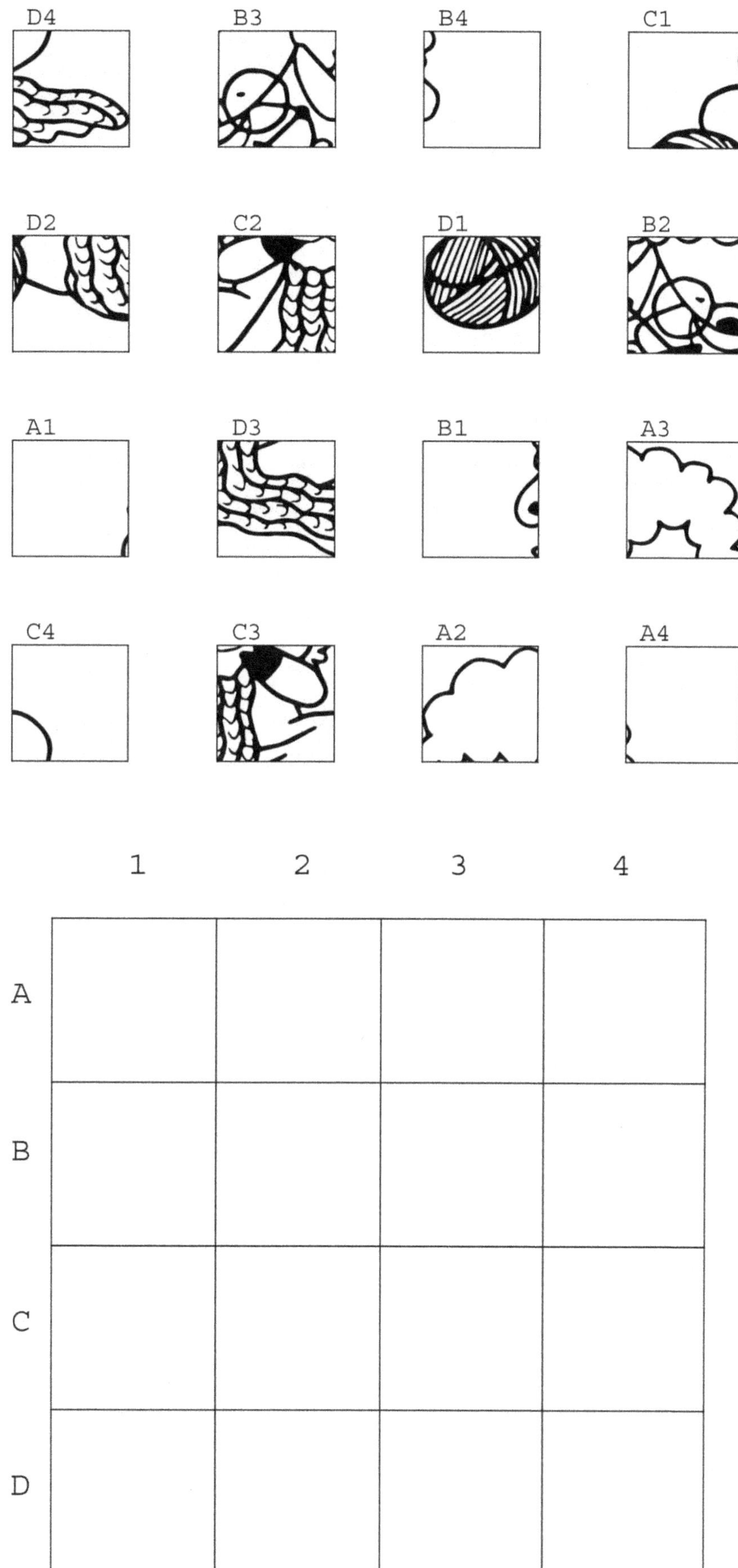

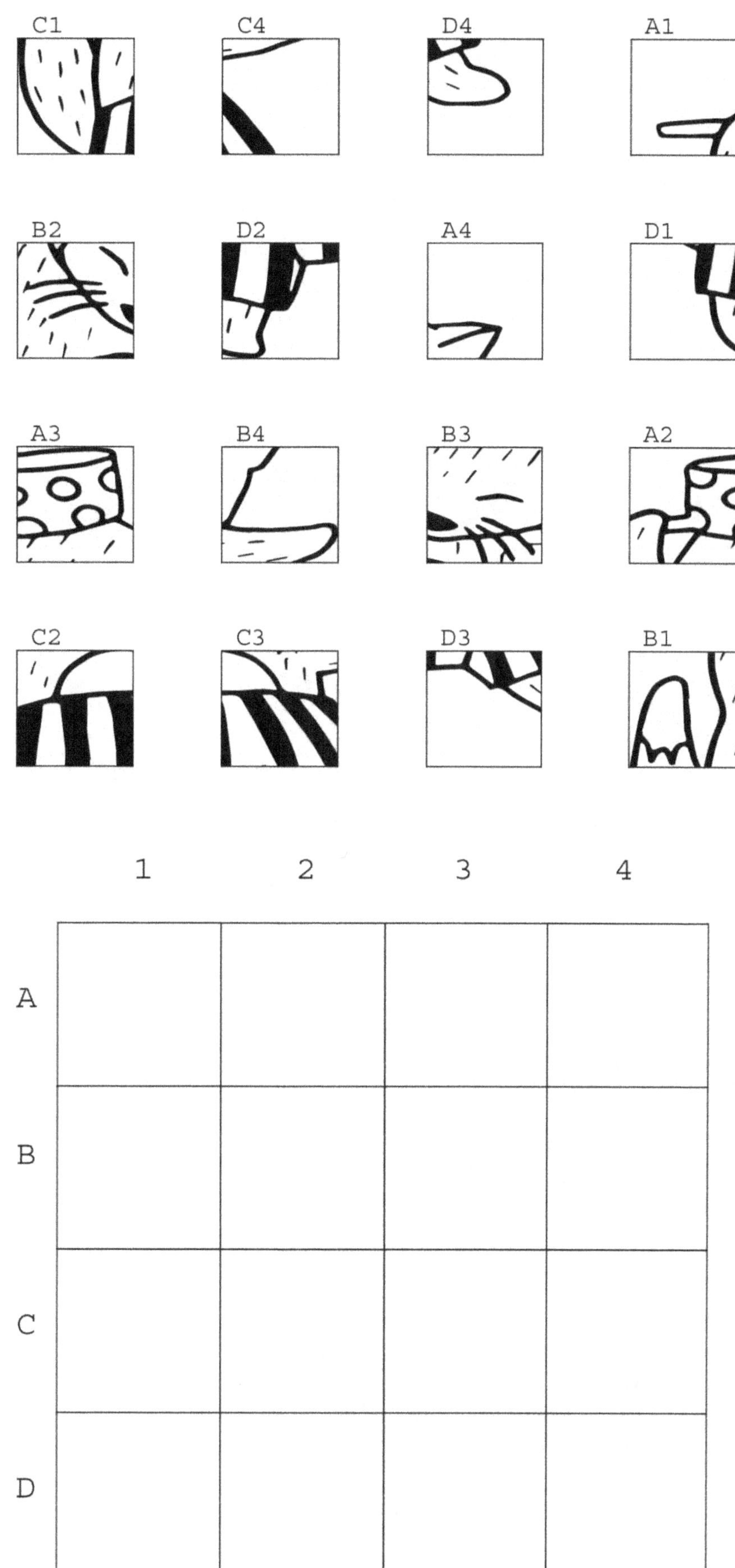

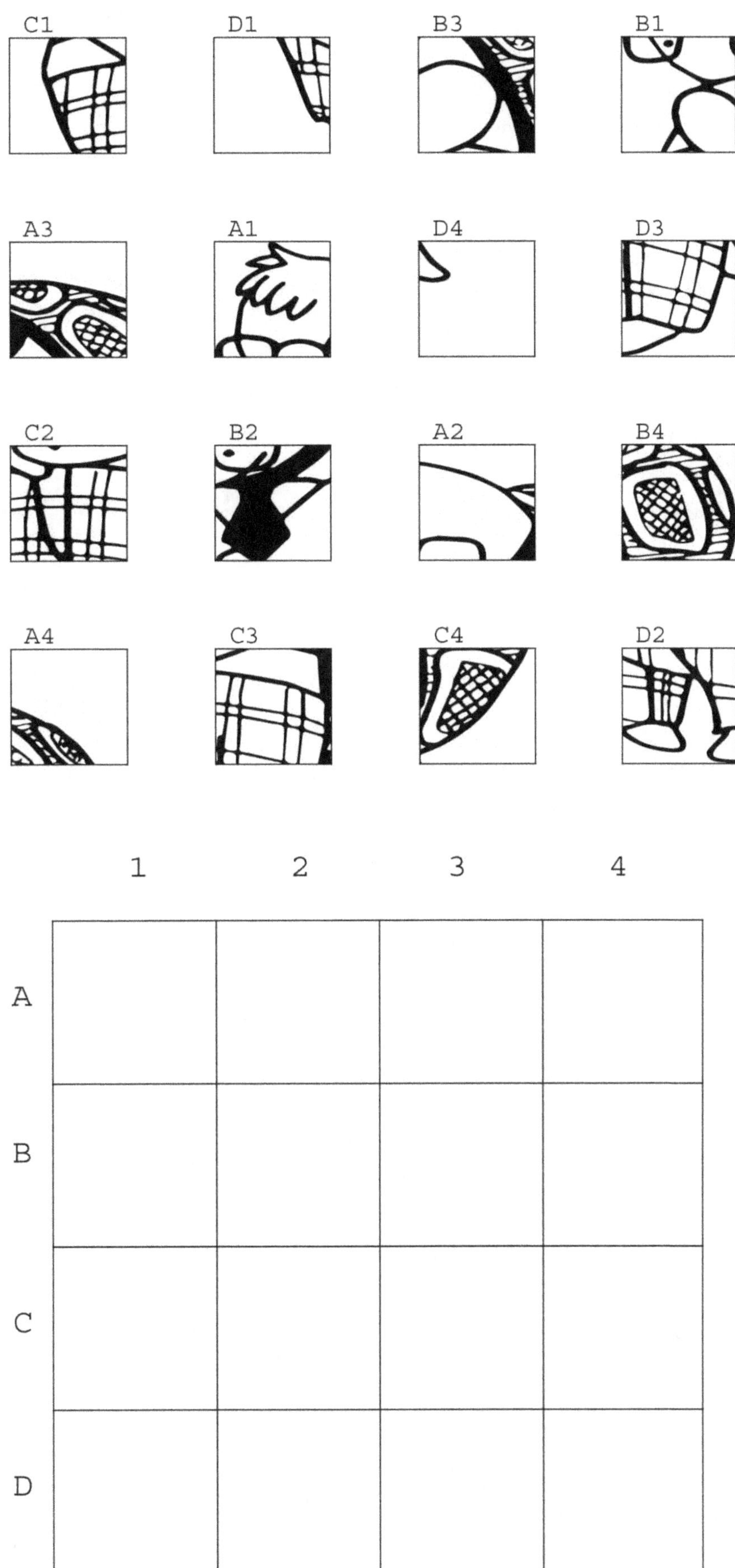

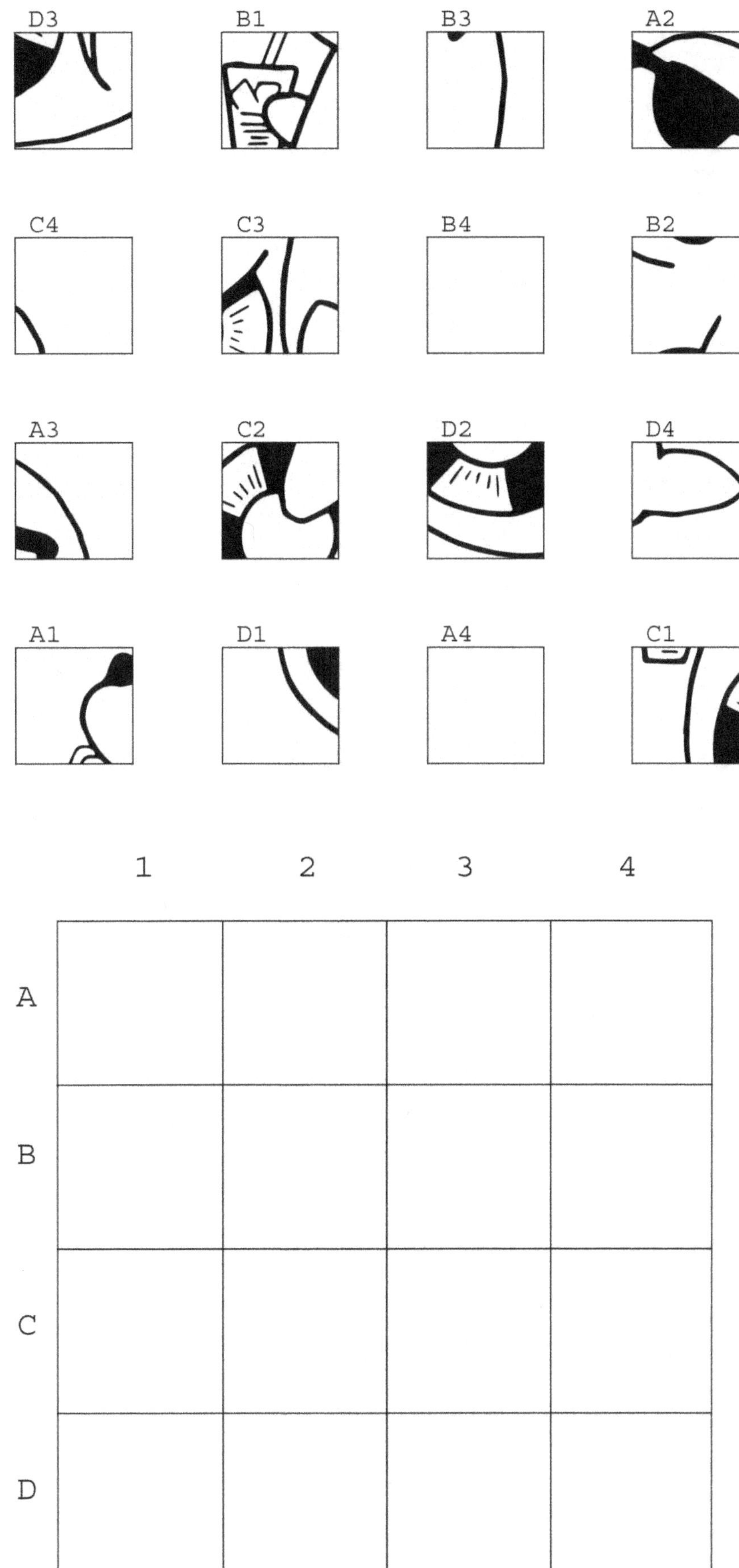

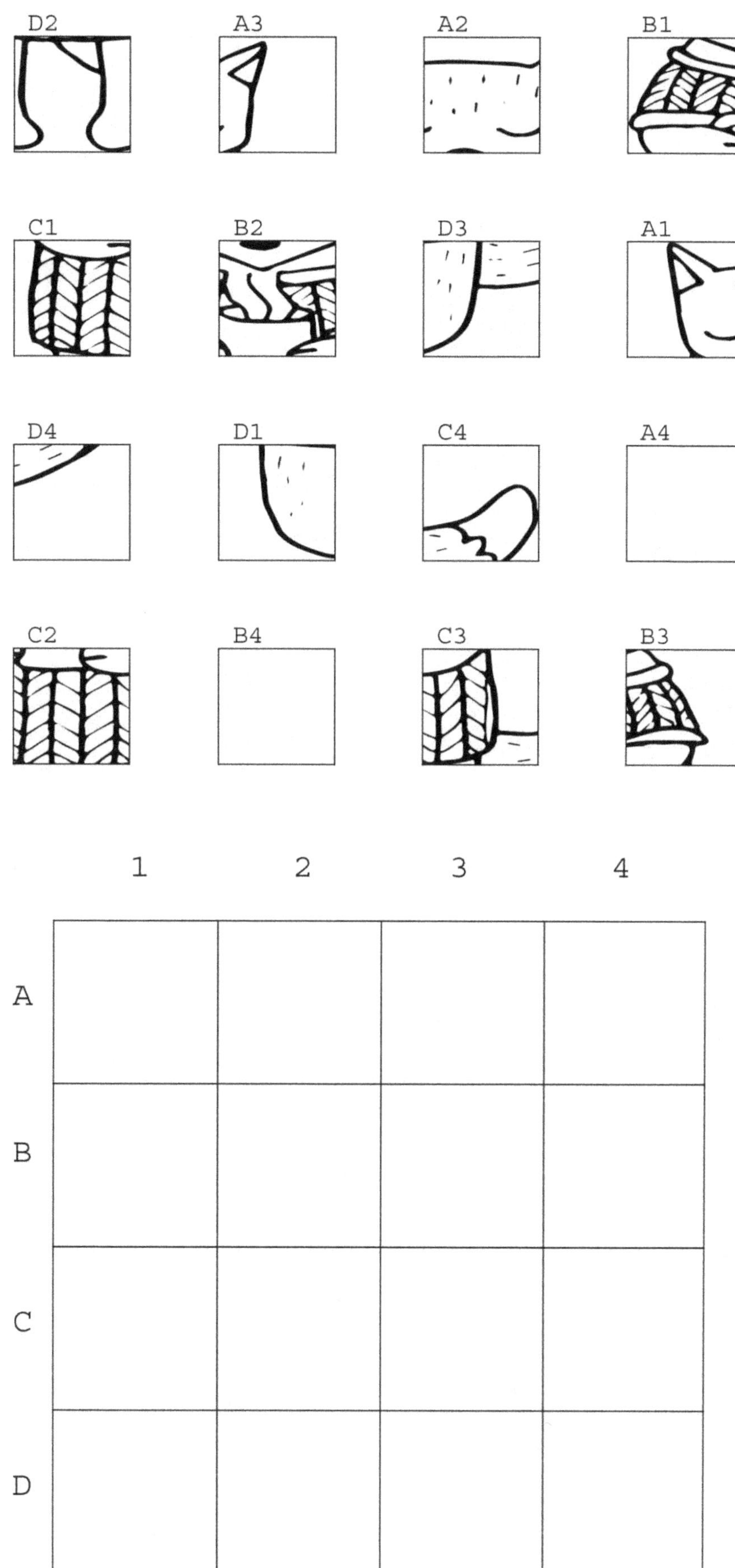

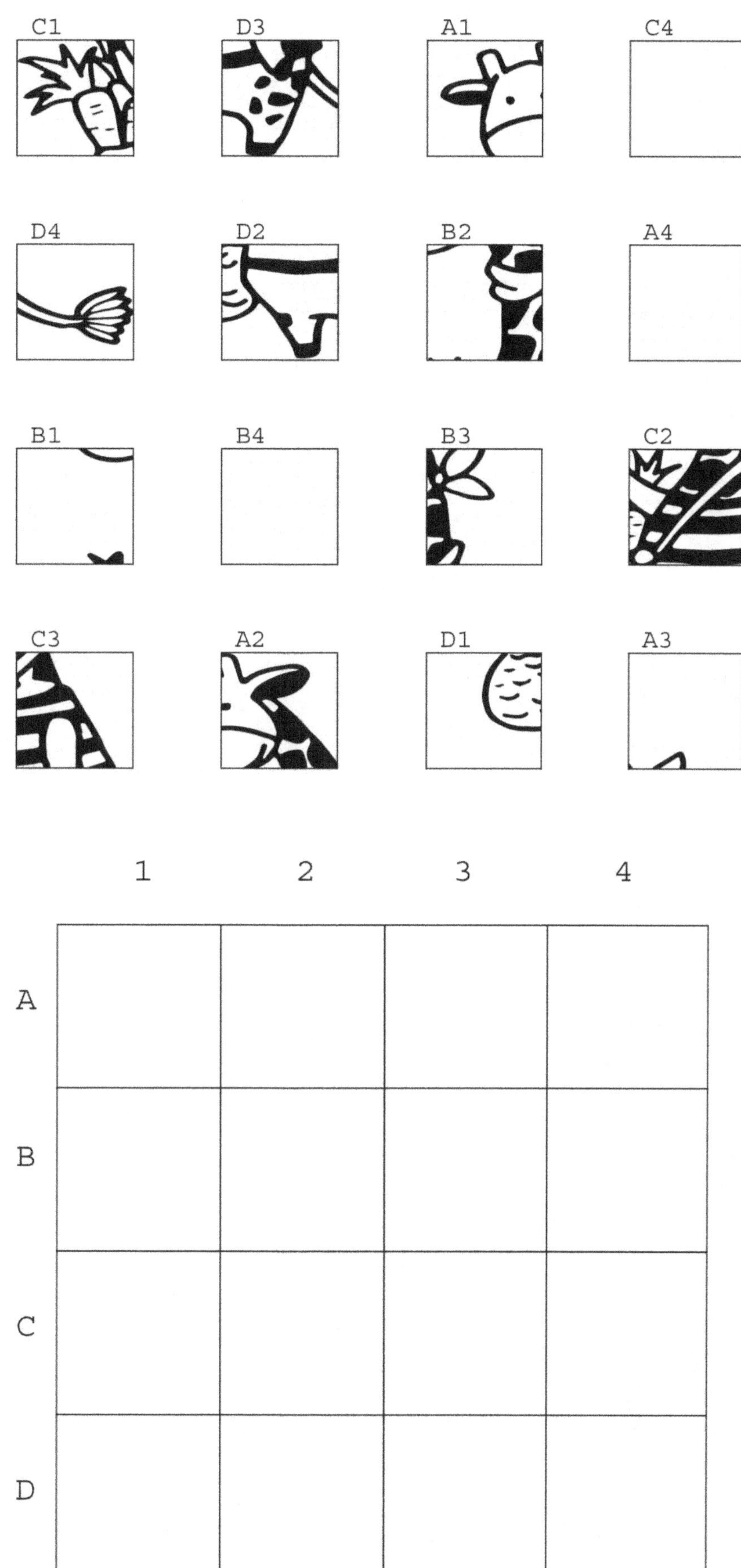

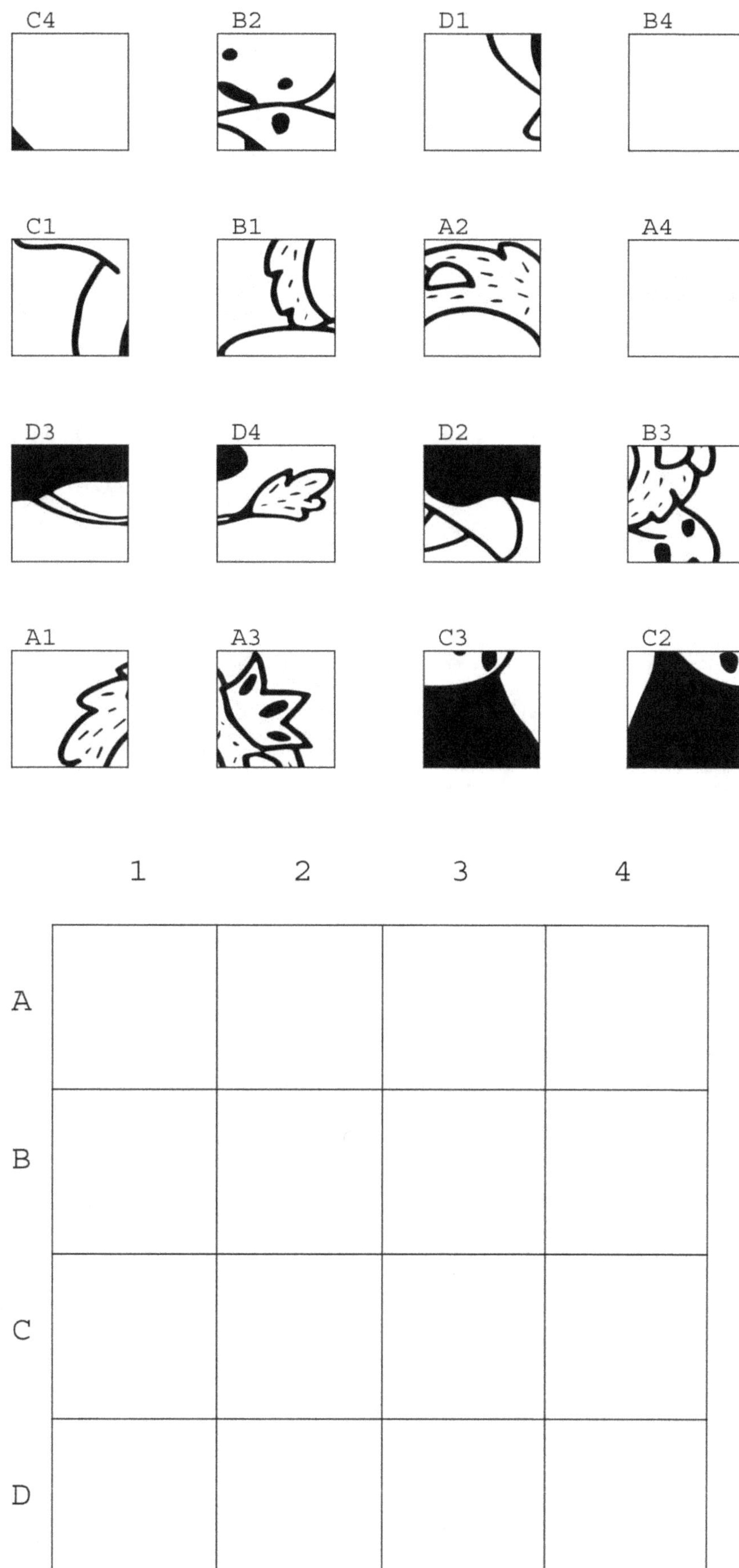

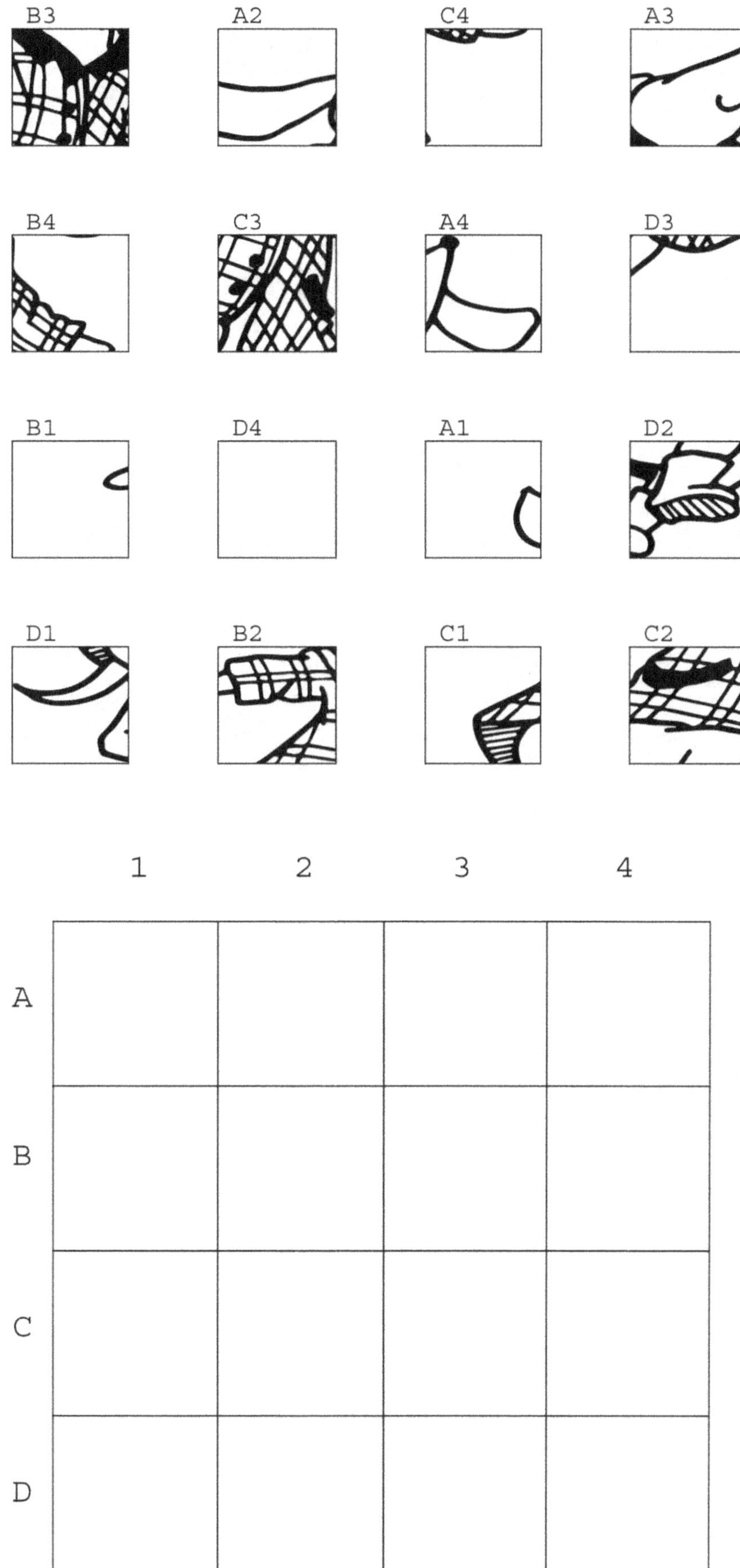

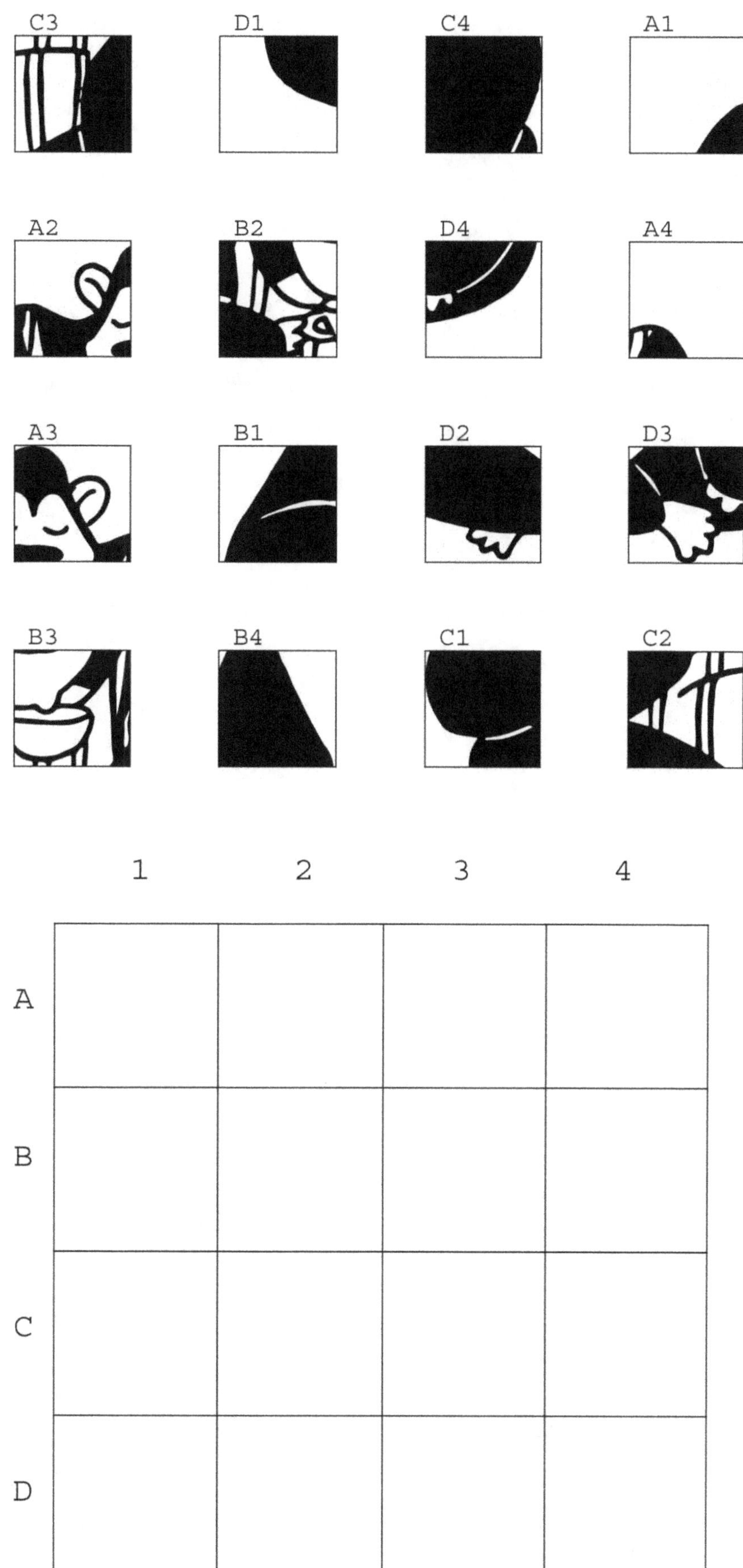

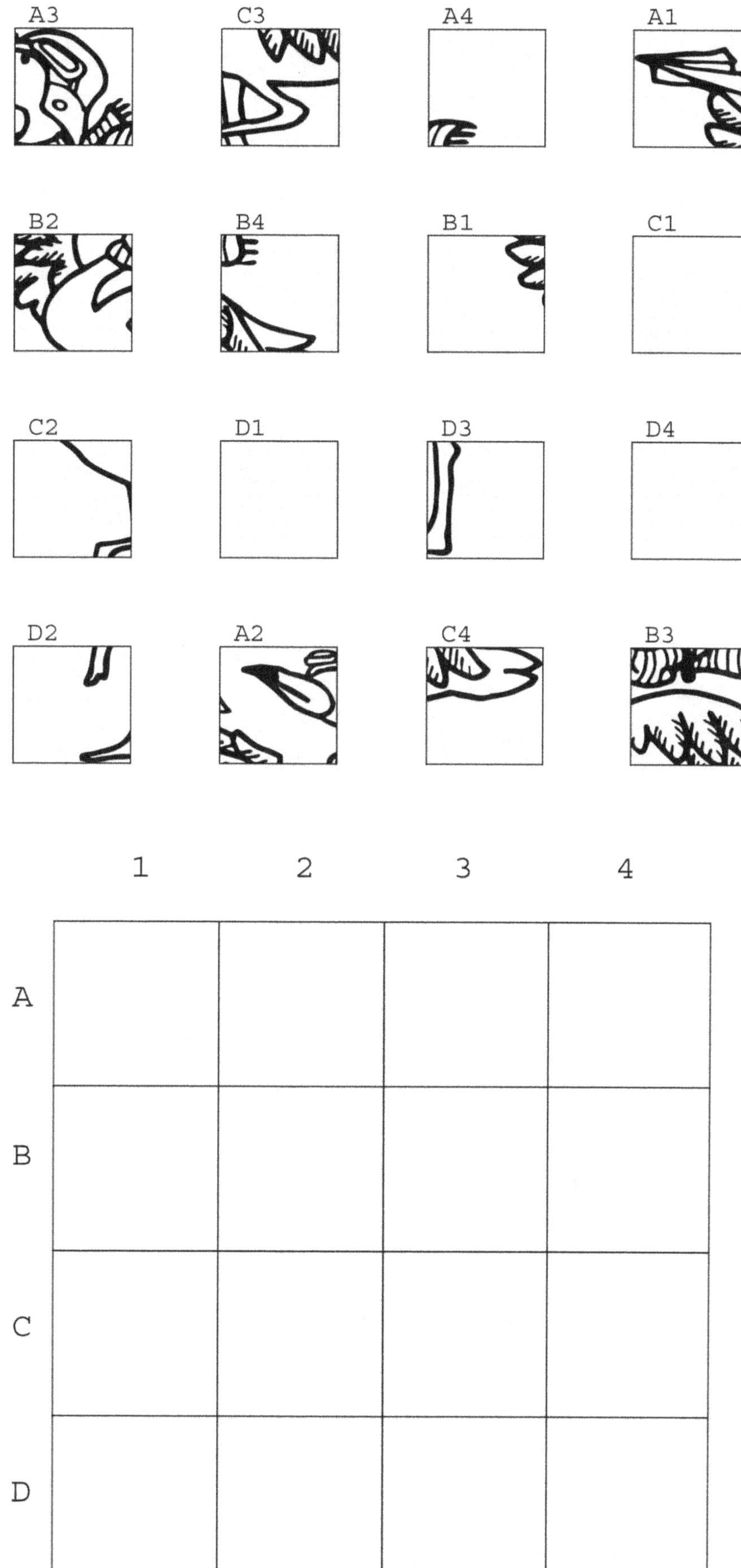

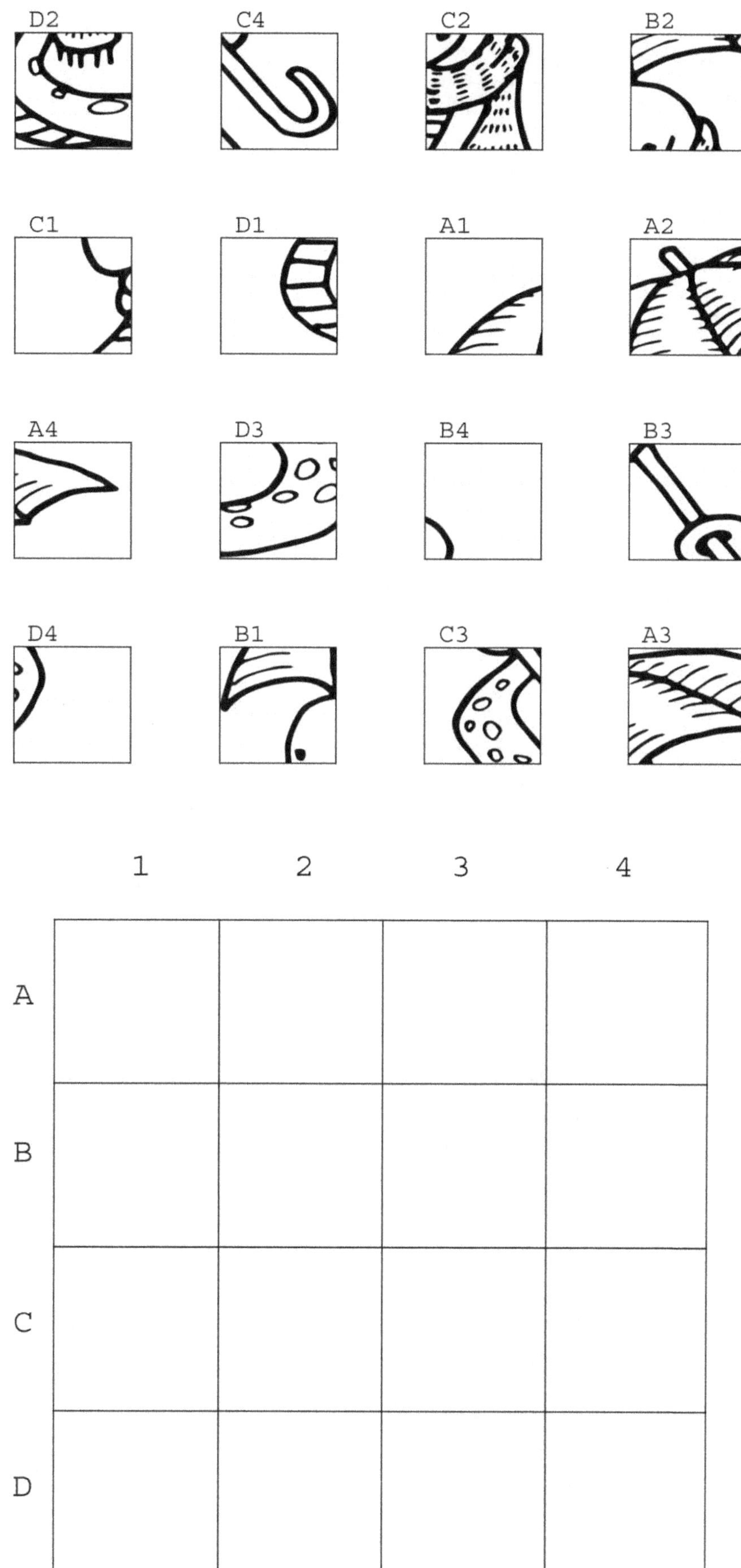

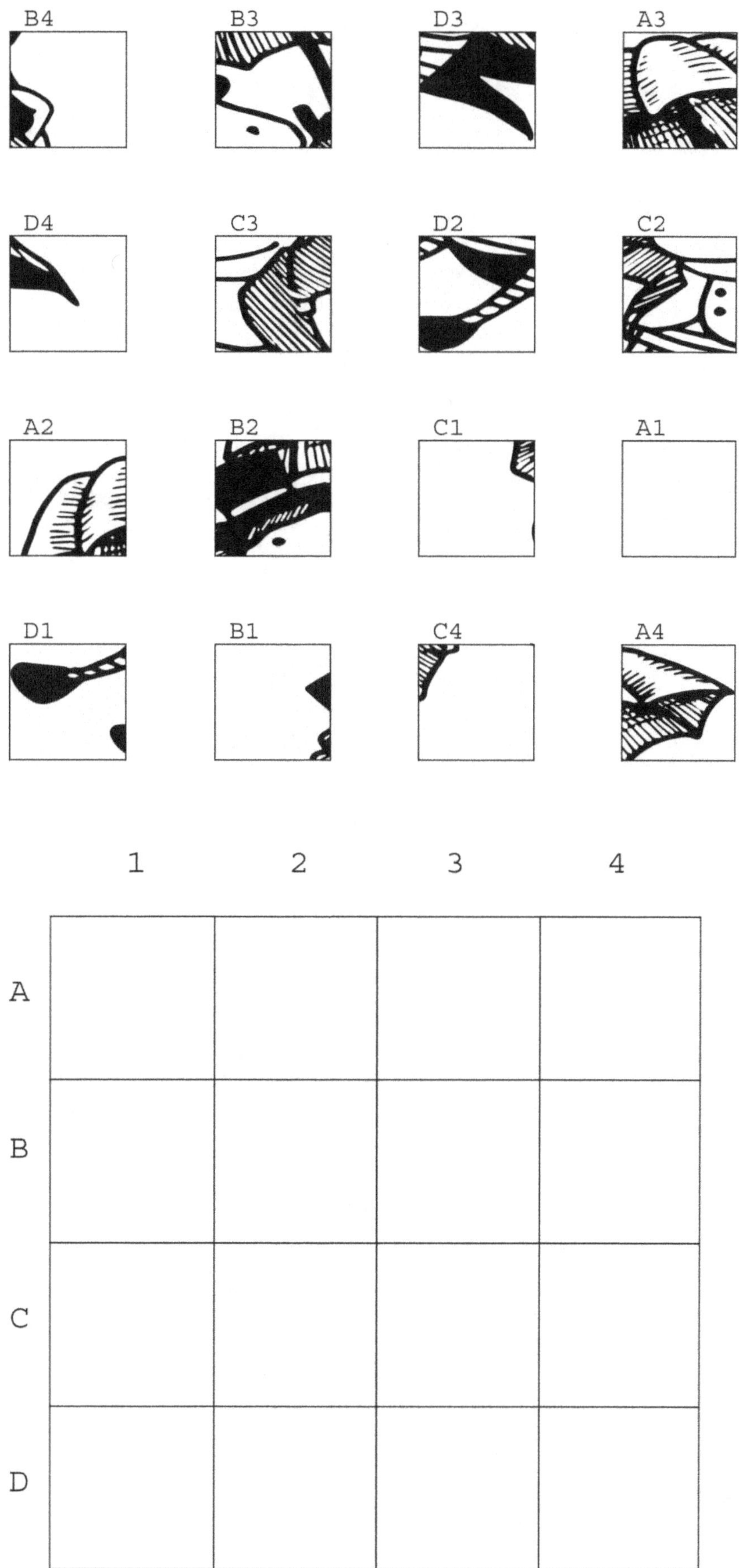

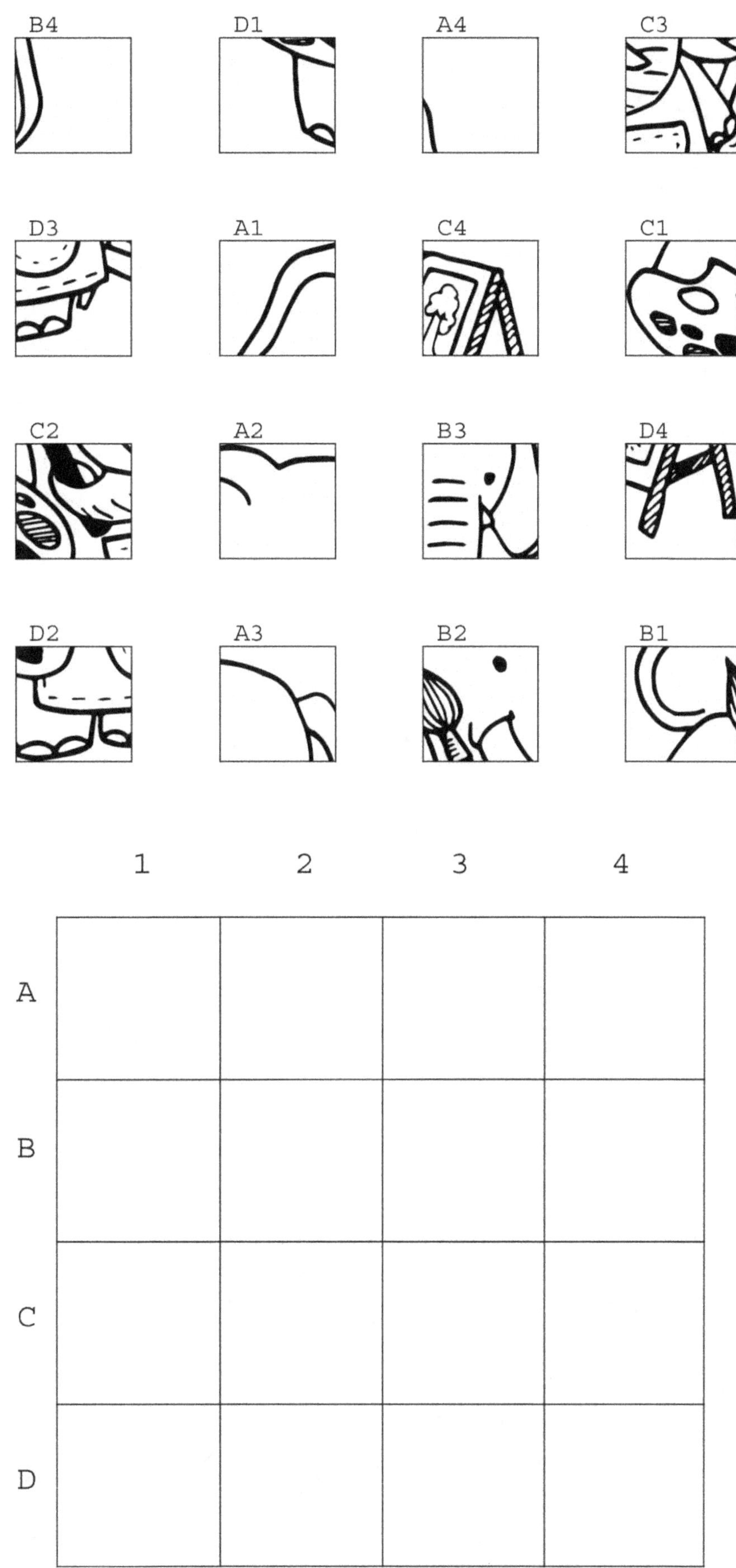

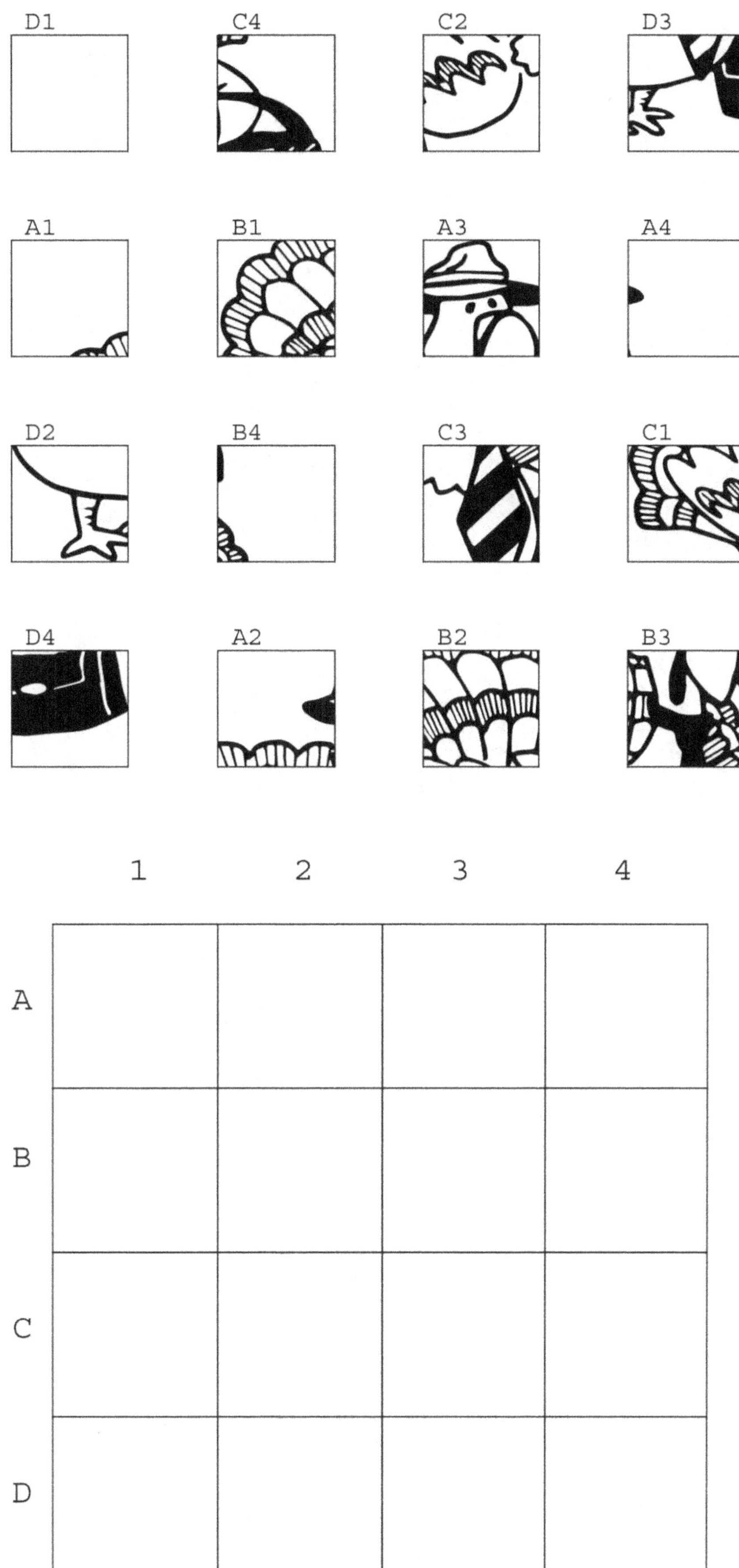

D1
C4
C2
D3
A1
B1
A3
A4
D2
B4
C3
C1
D4
A2
B2
B3
1
2
3
4
A
B
C
D

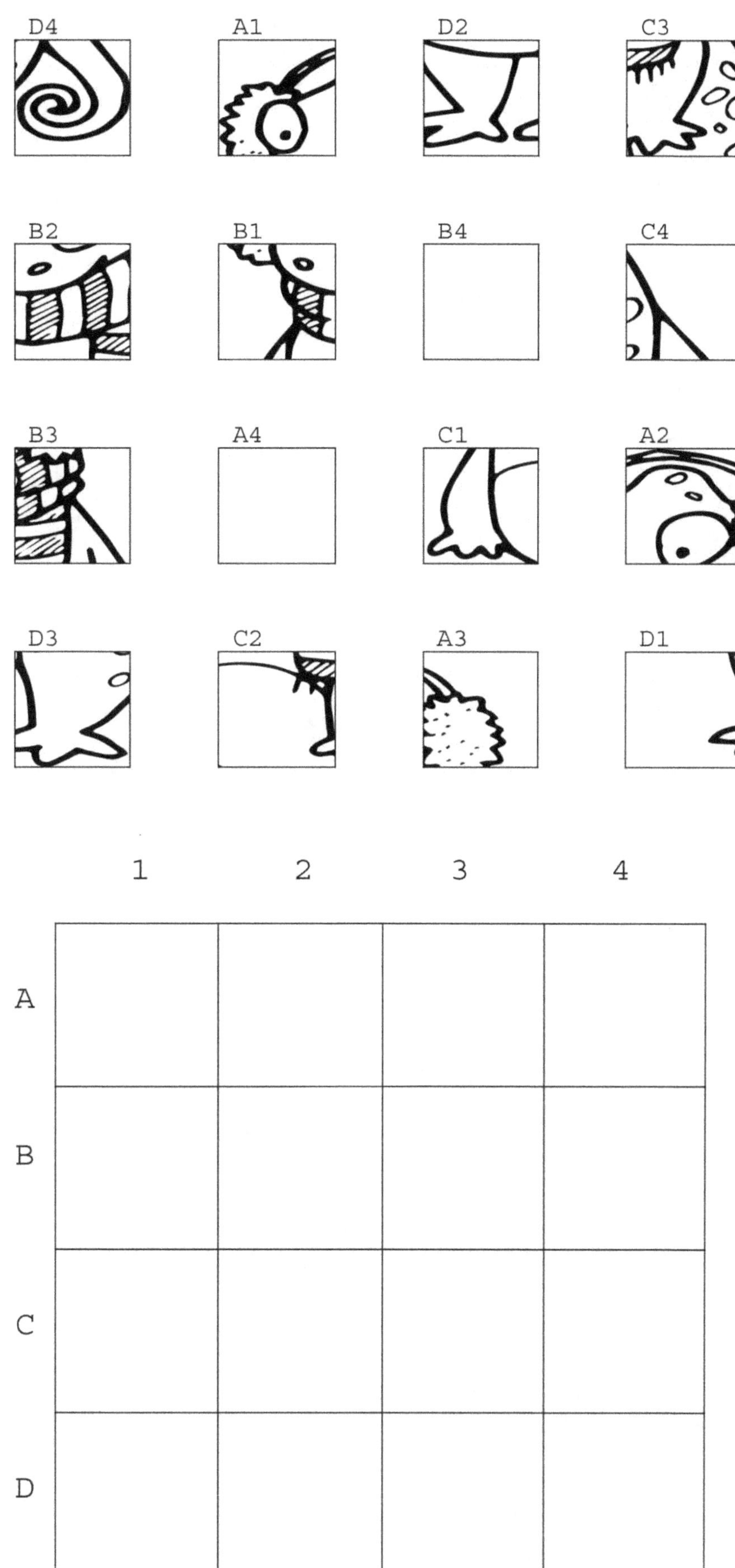

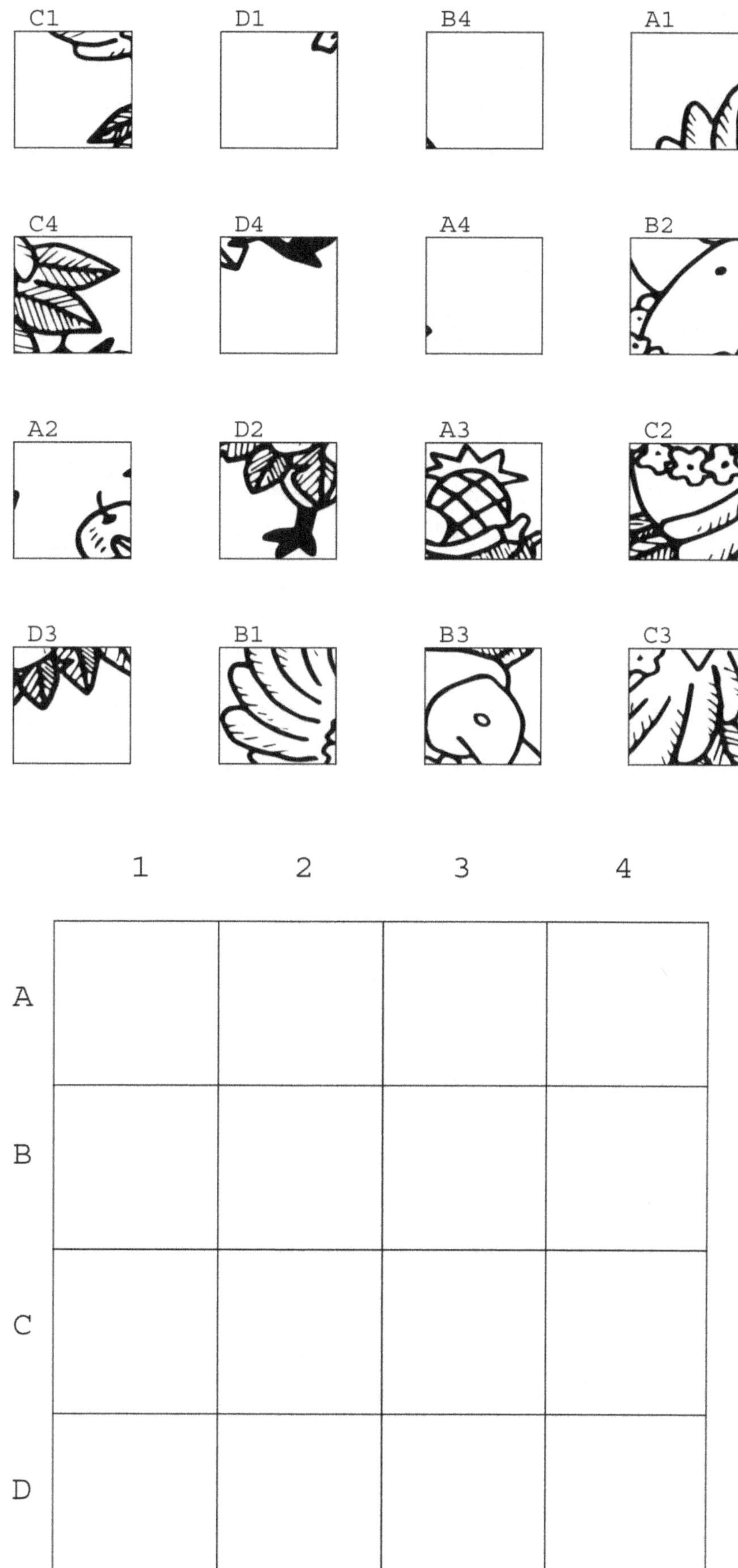

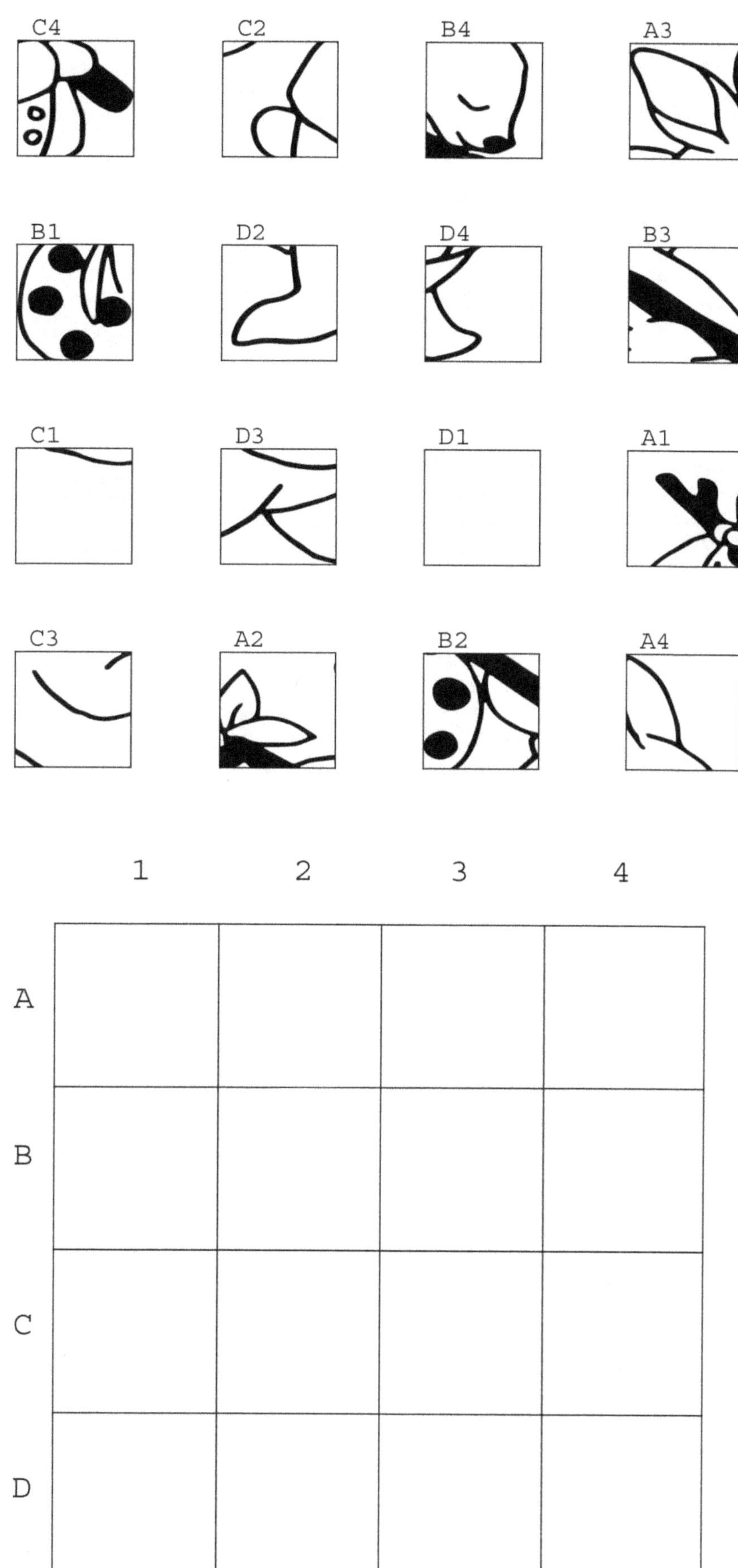

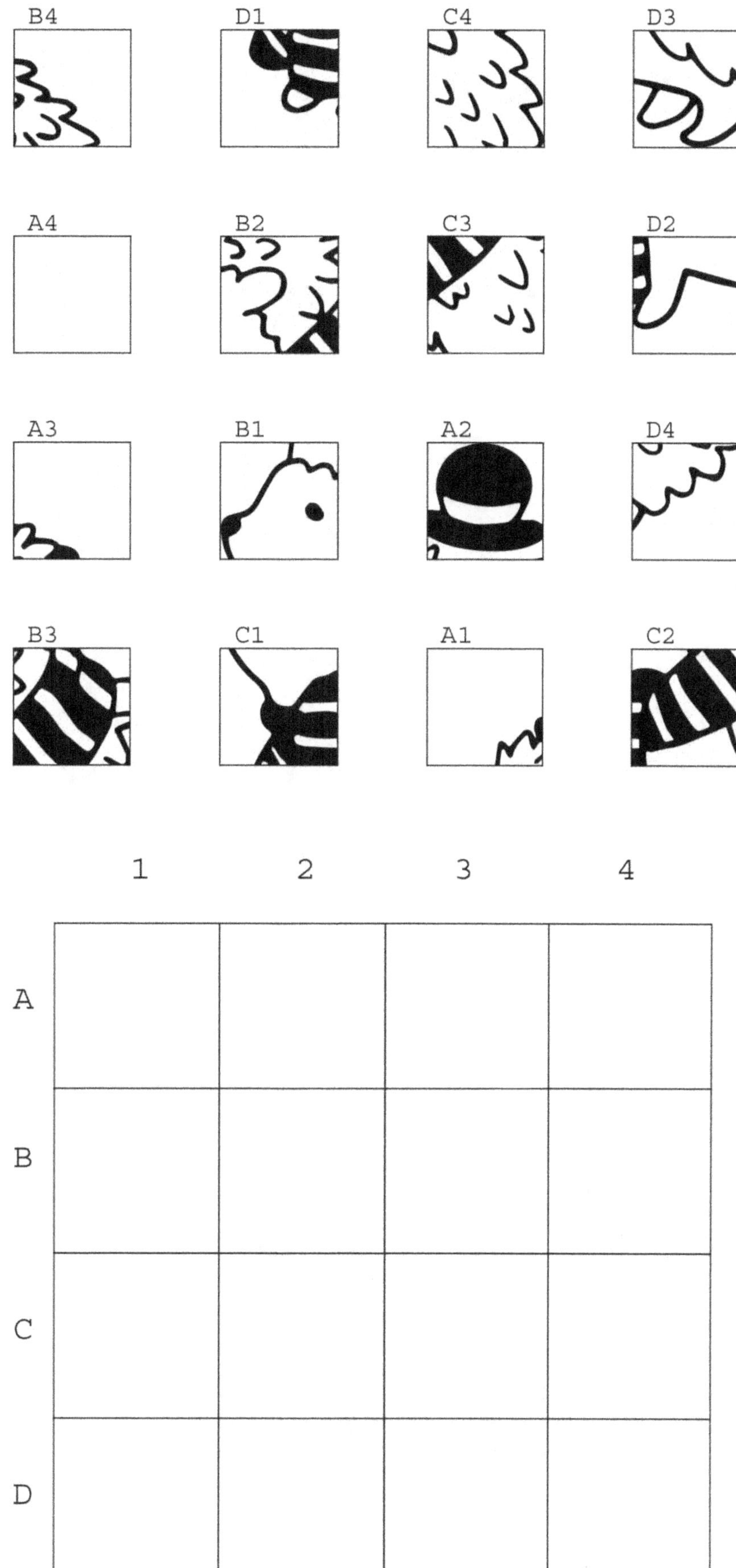

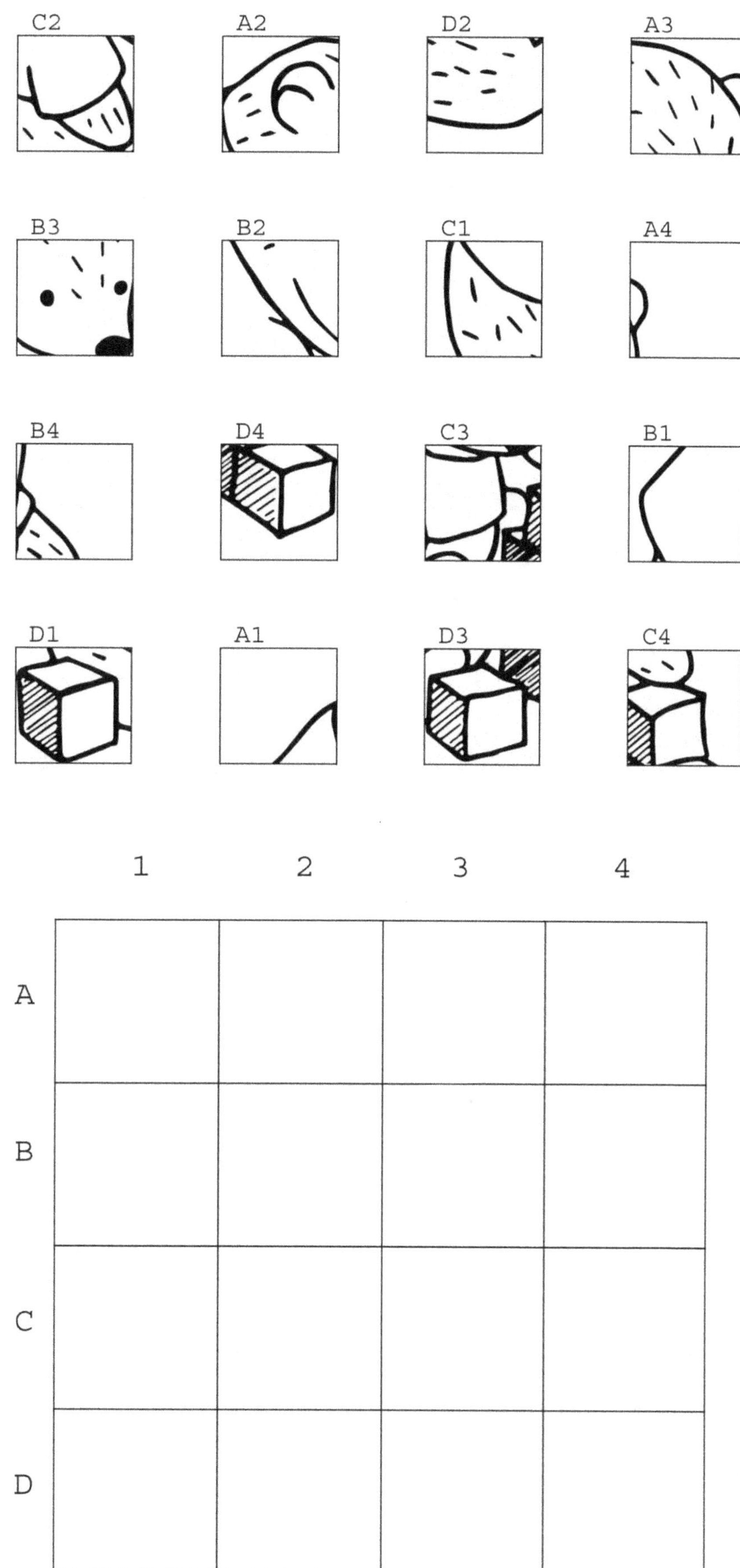

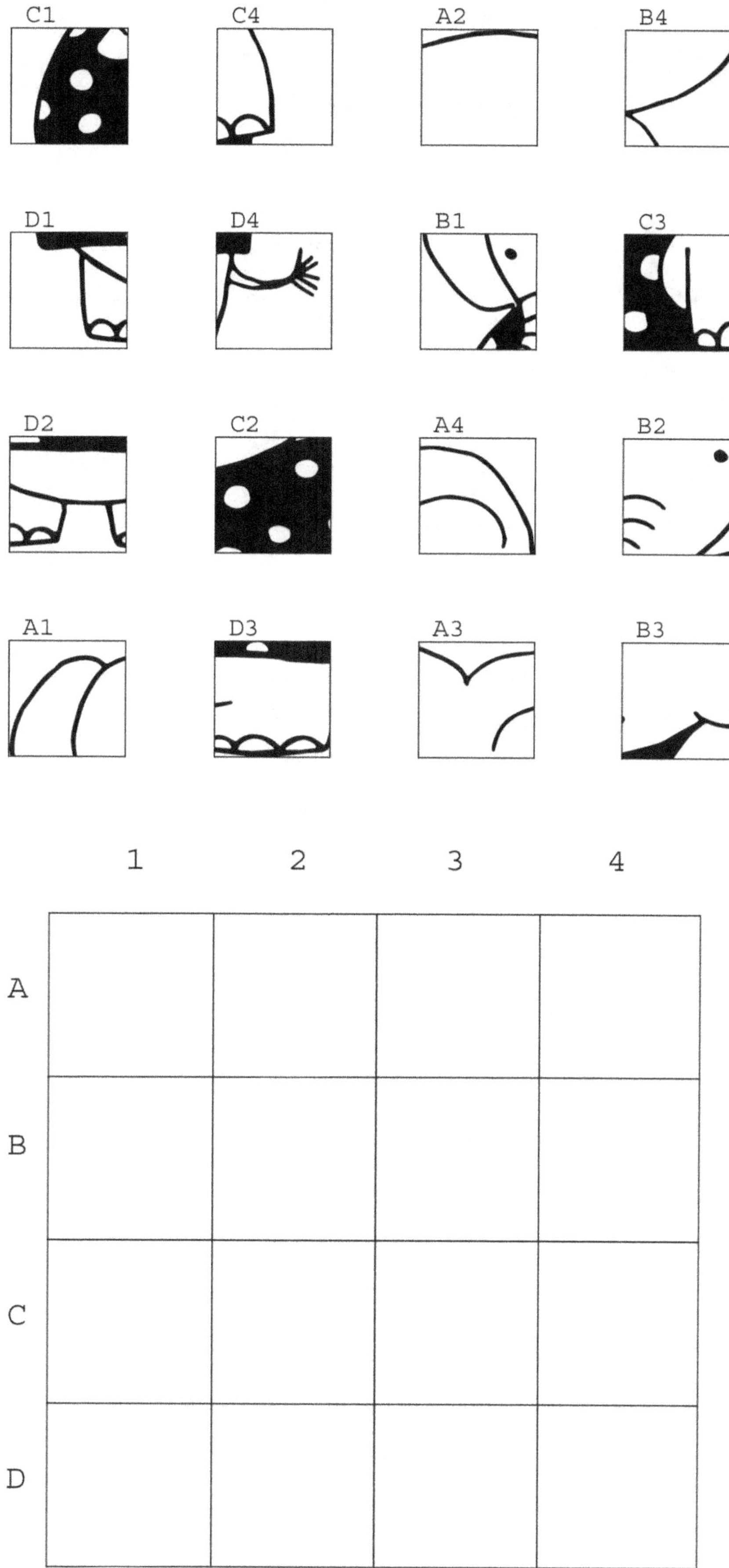

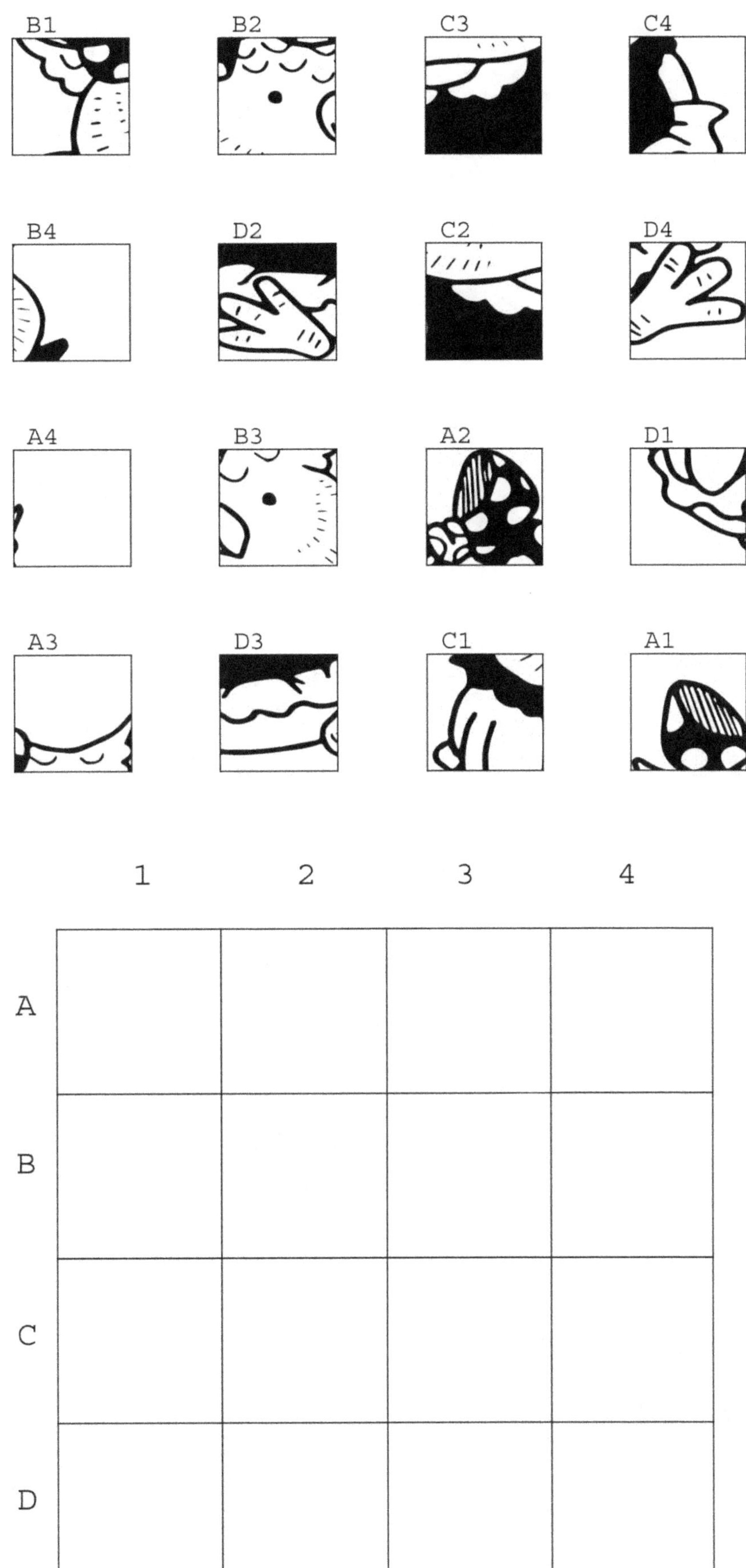

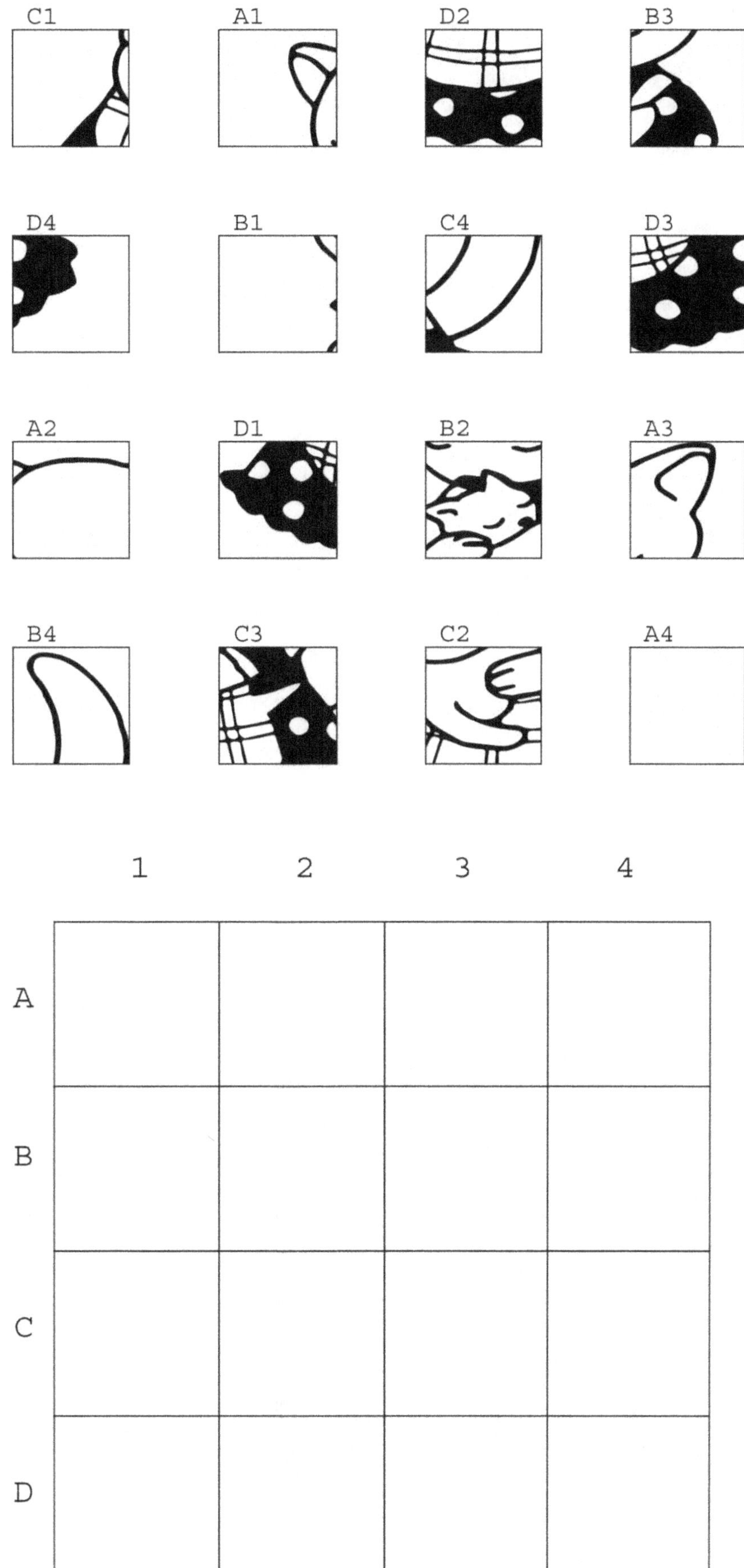

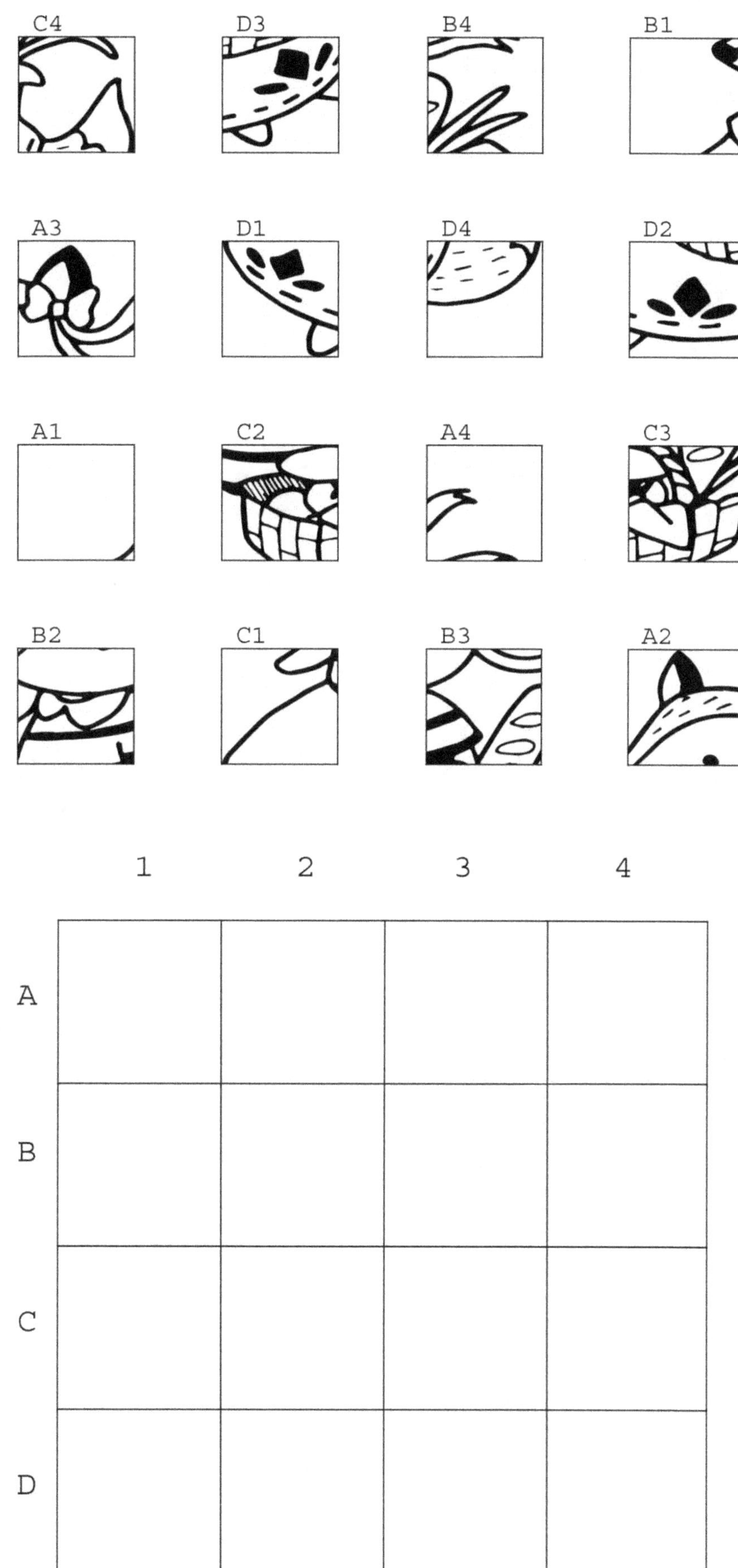

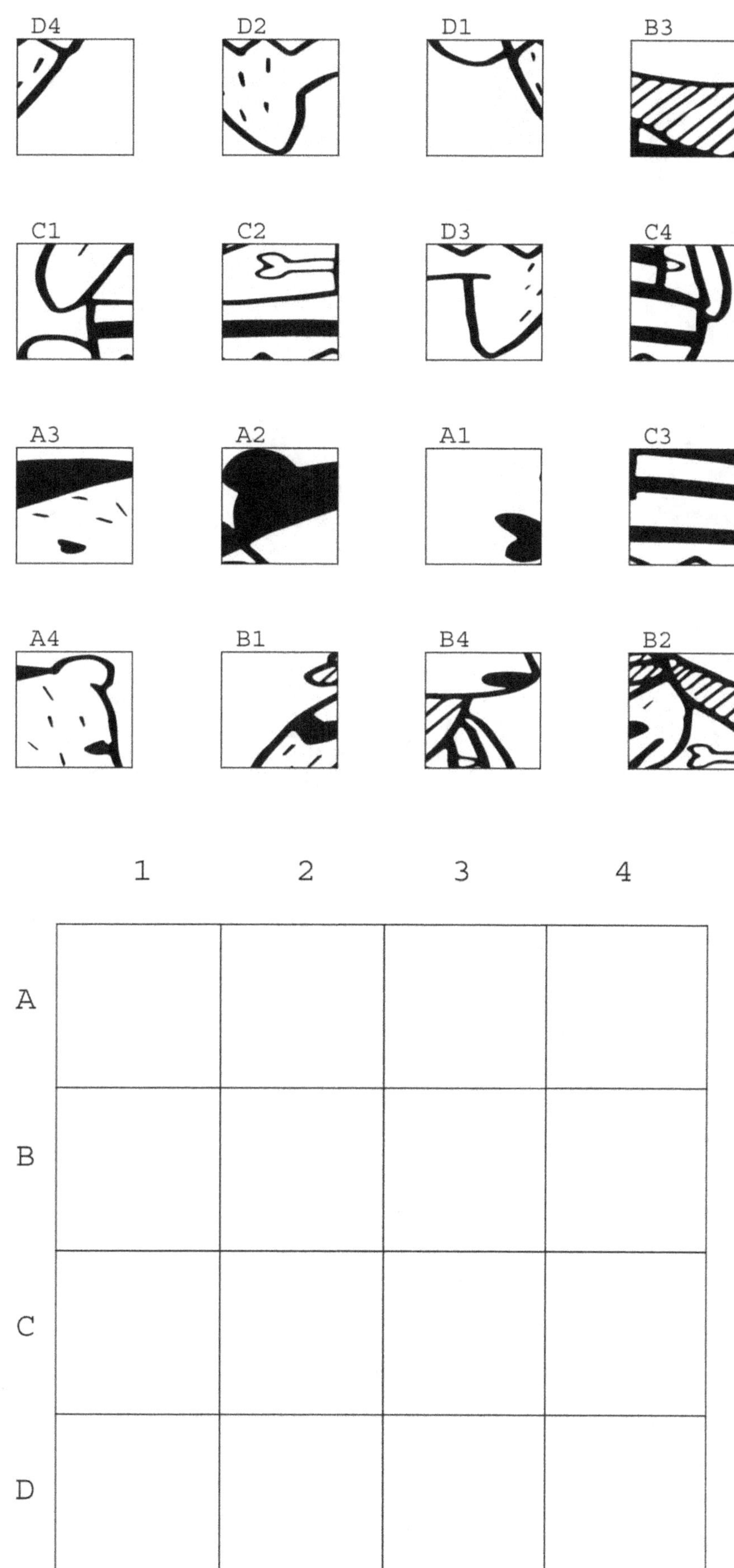

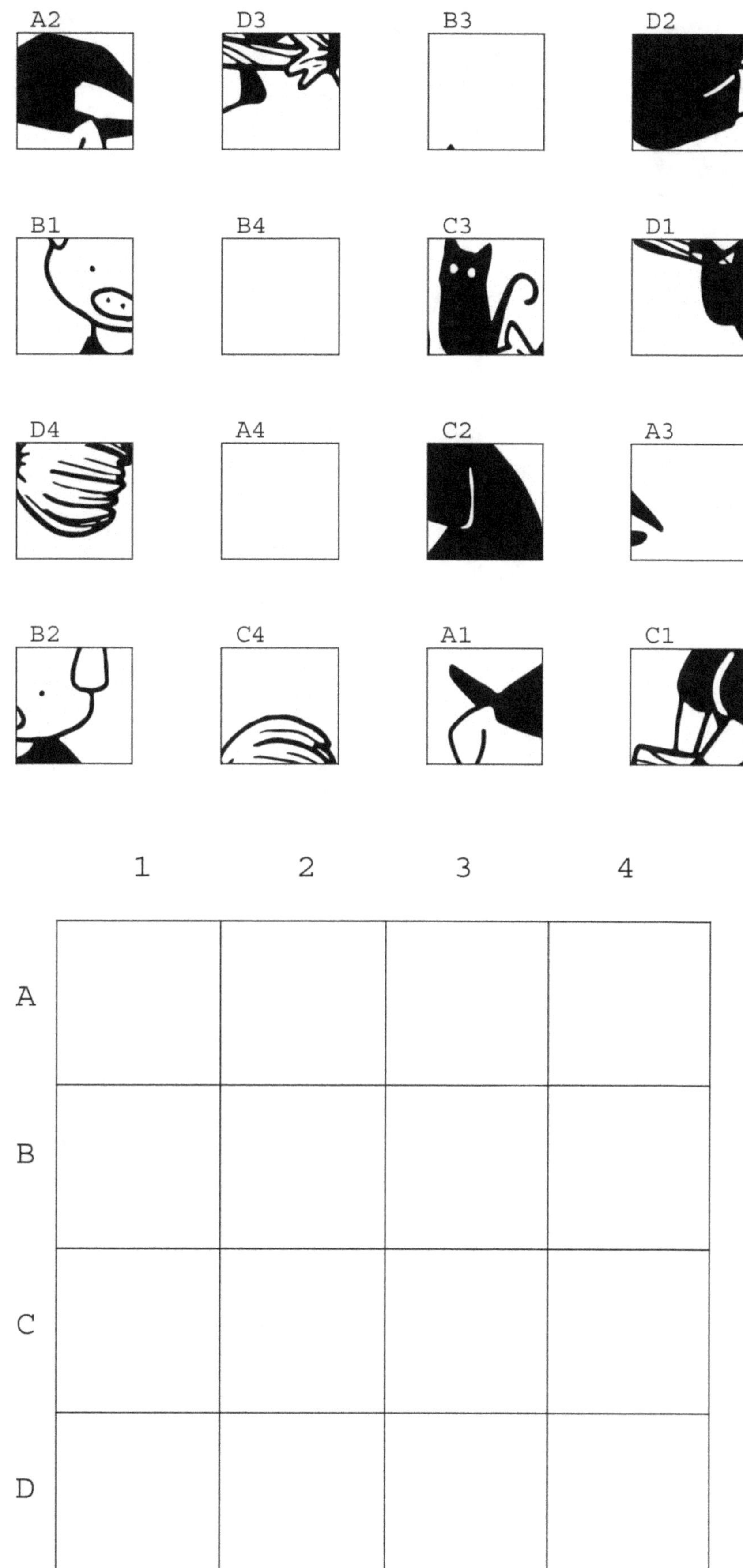

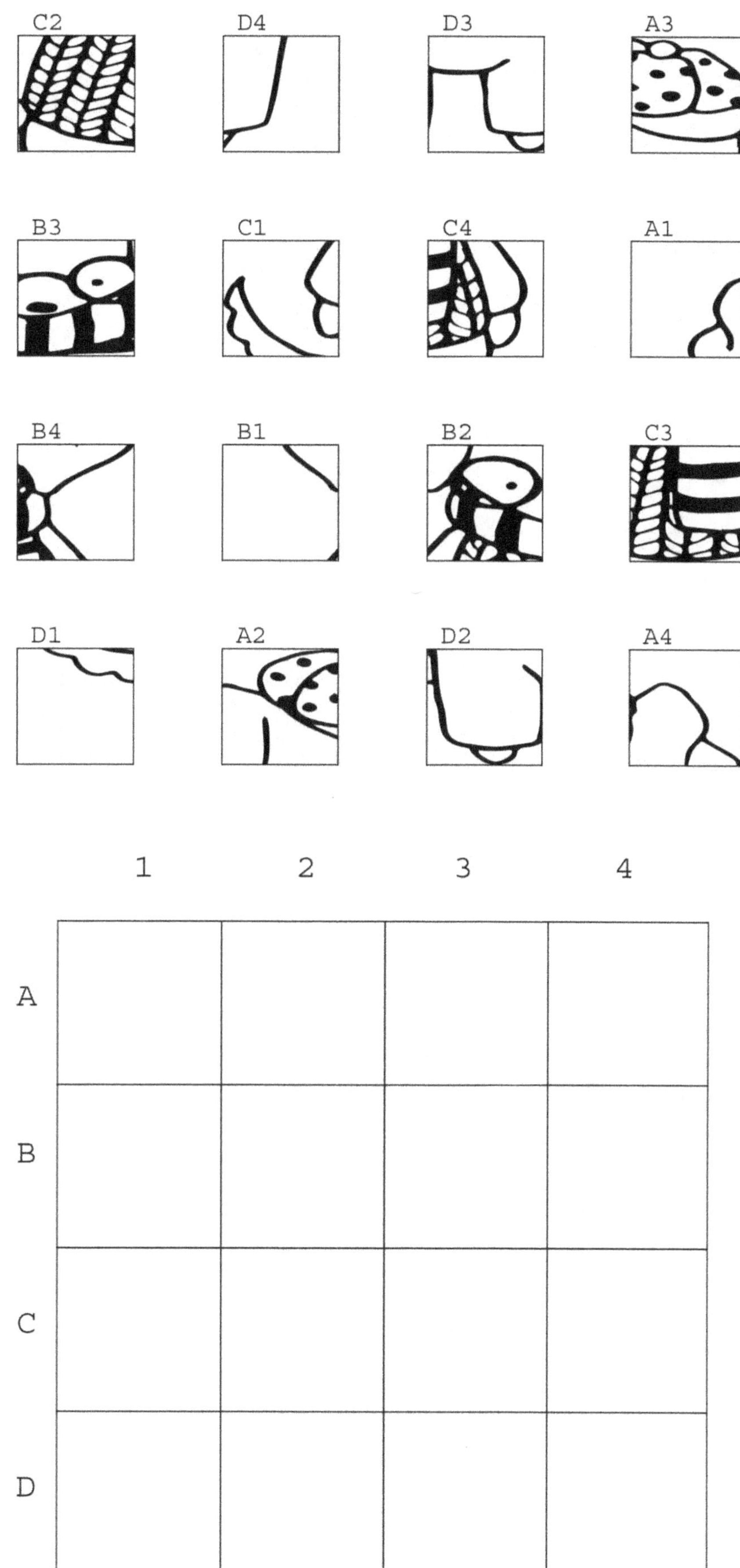

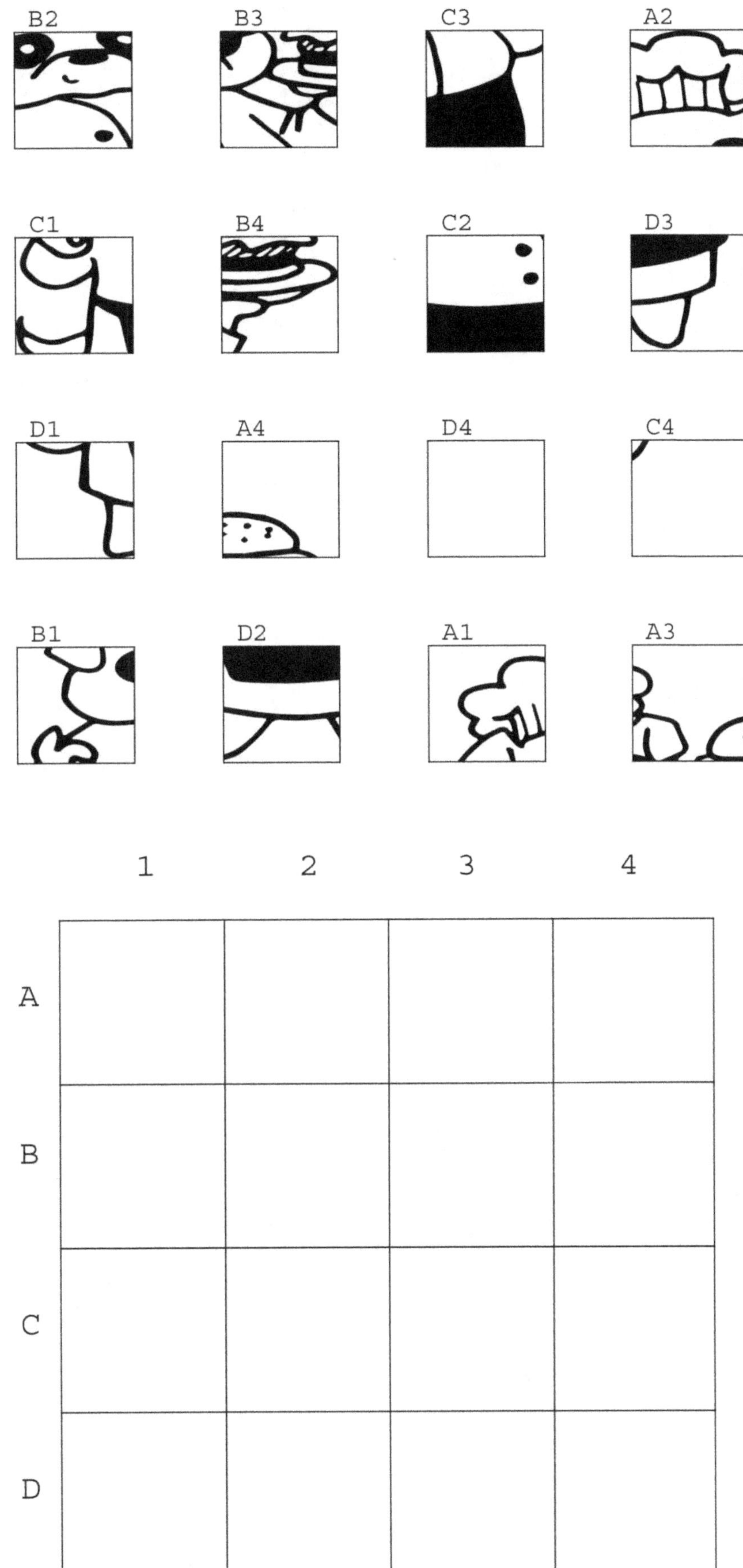

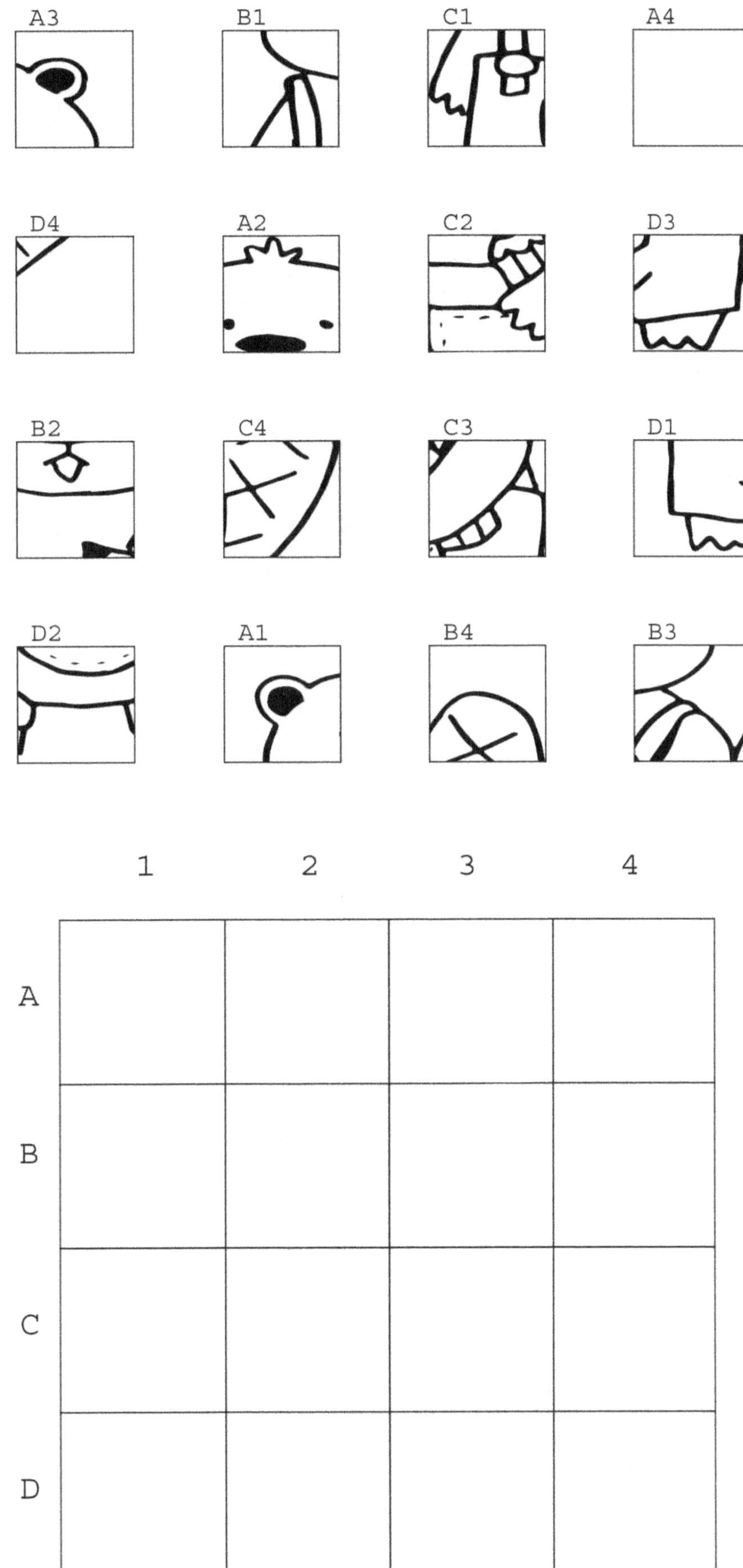

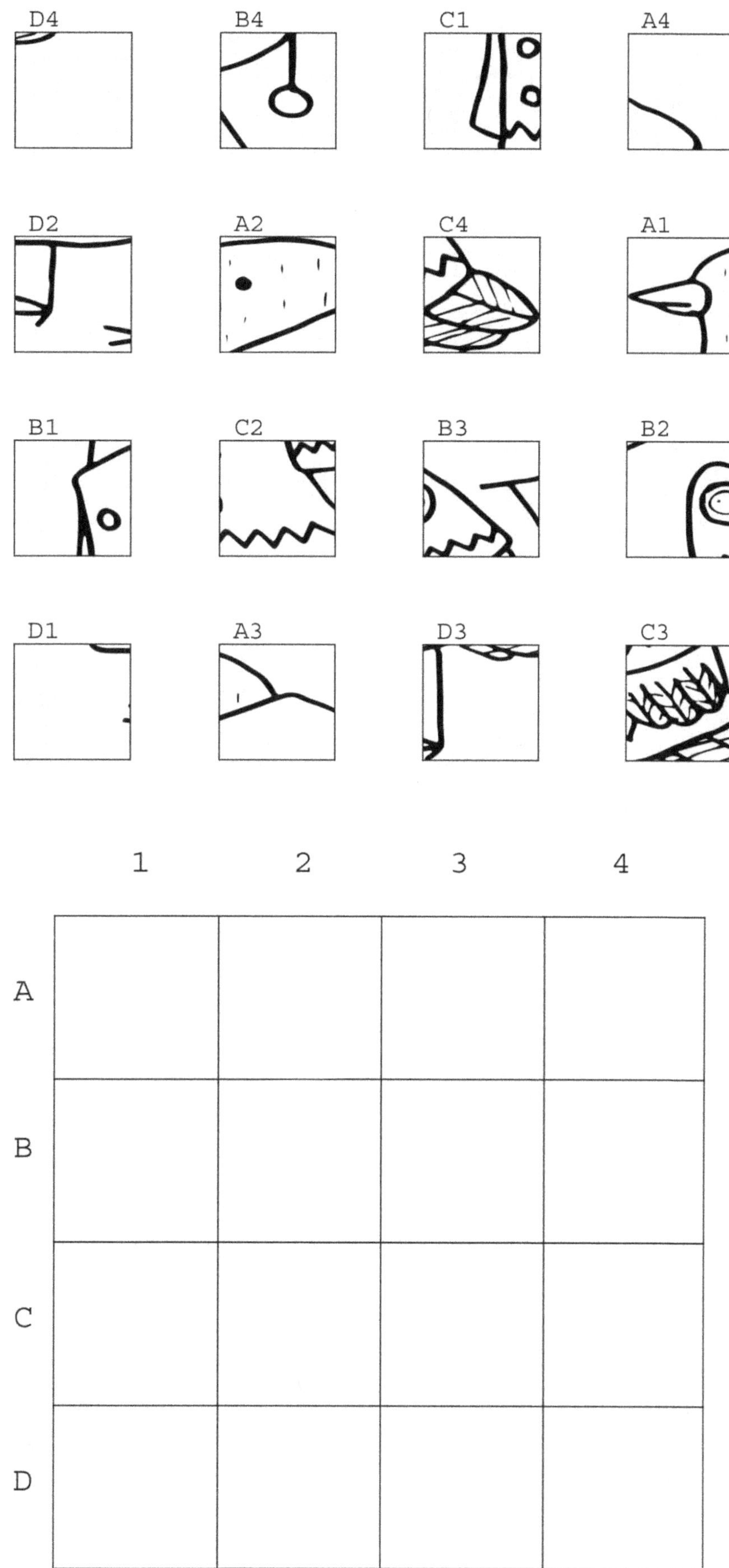

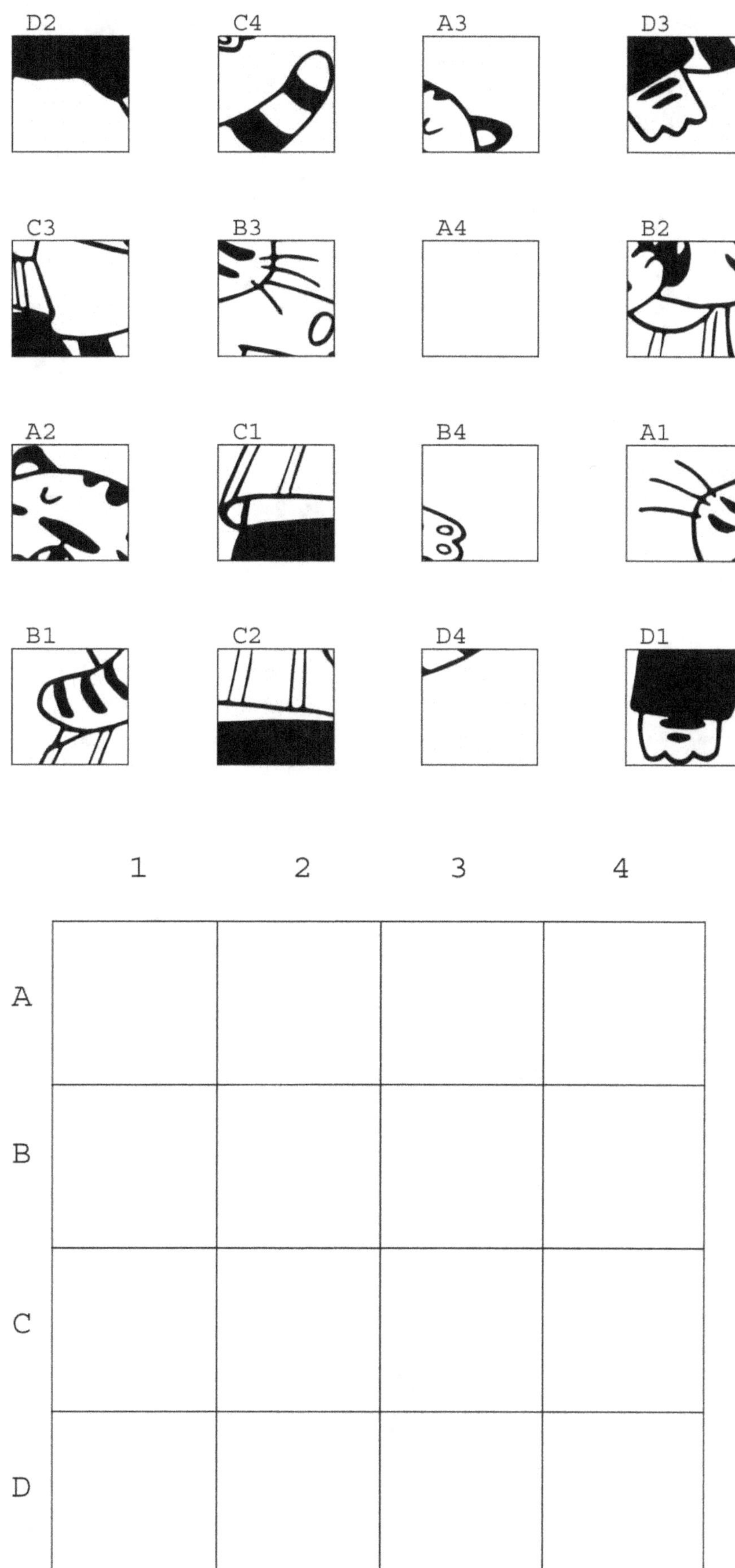

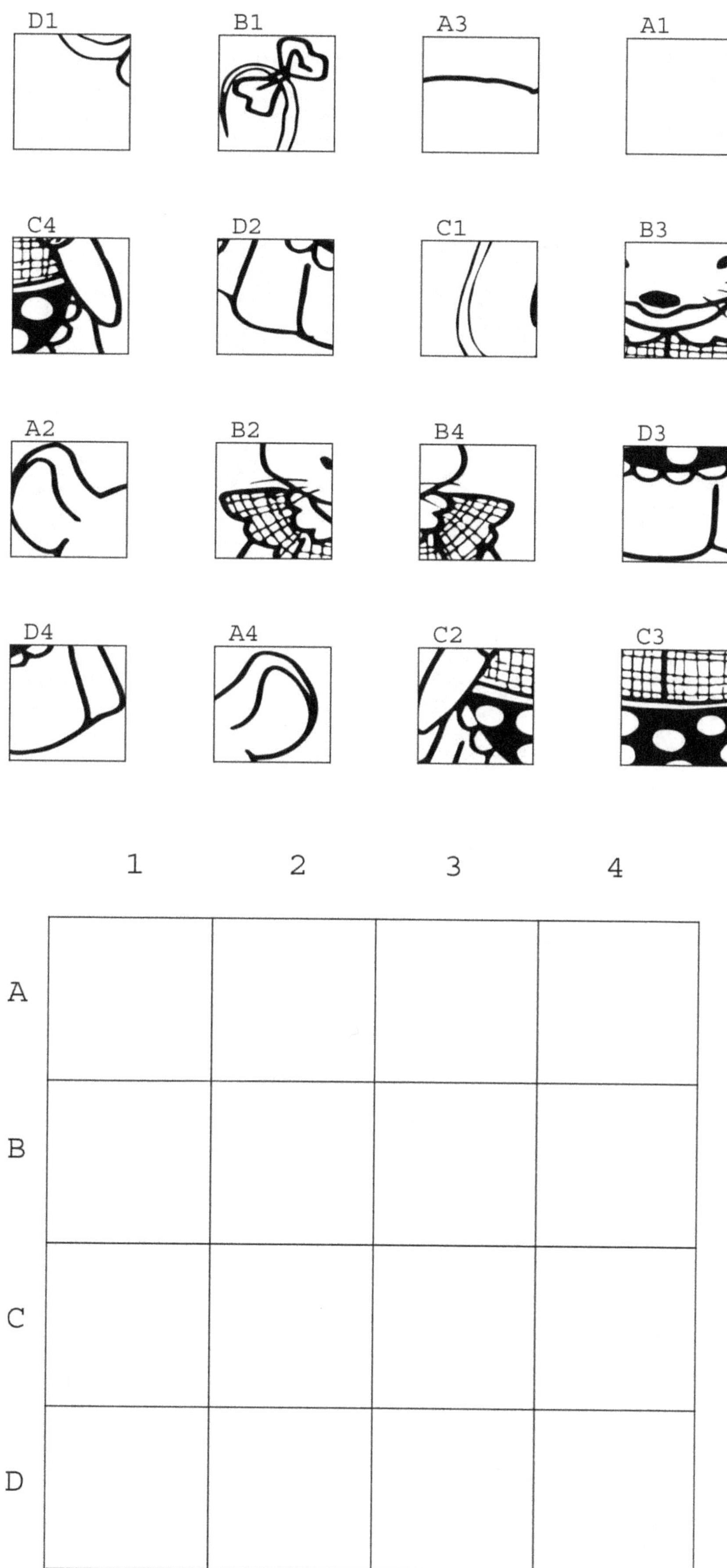

D1
B1
A3
A1
C4
D2
C1
B3
A2
B2
B4
D3
D4
A4
C2
C3
1   2   3   4
A
B
C
D

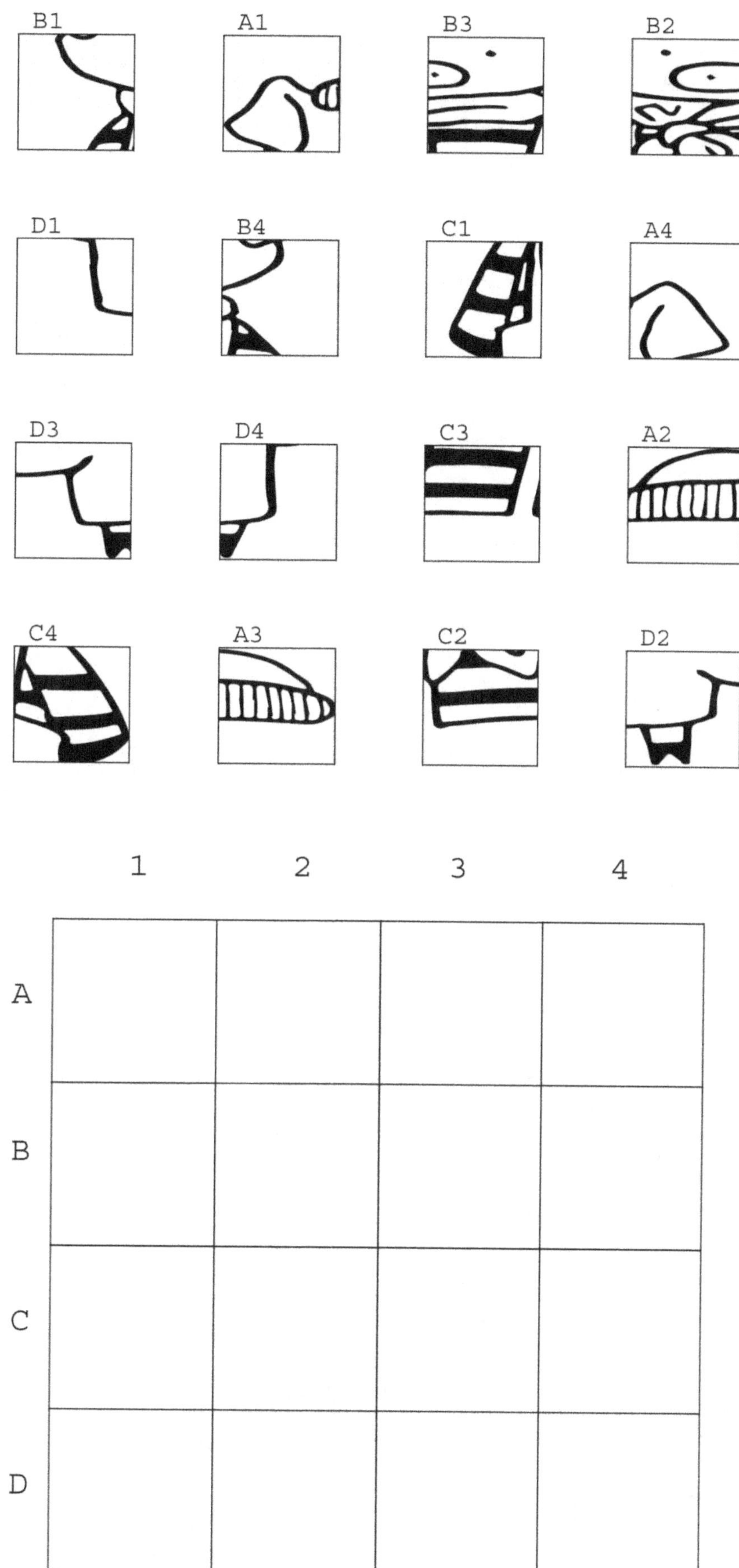

Thank you for completing our book! We appreciate your time and hope you enjoyed the experience. If you're up for more creative challenges, check out our other Pik-Jig books. Explore new grids and dive into the joy of artistic discovery. Happy drawing!

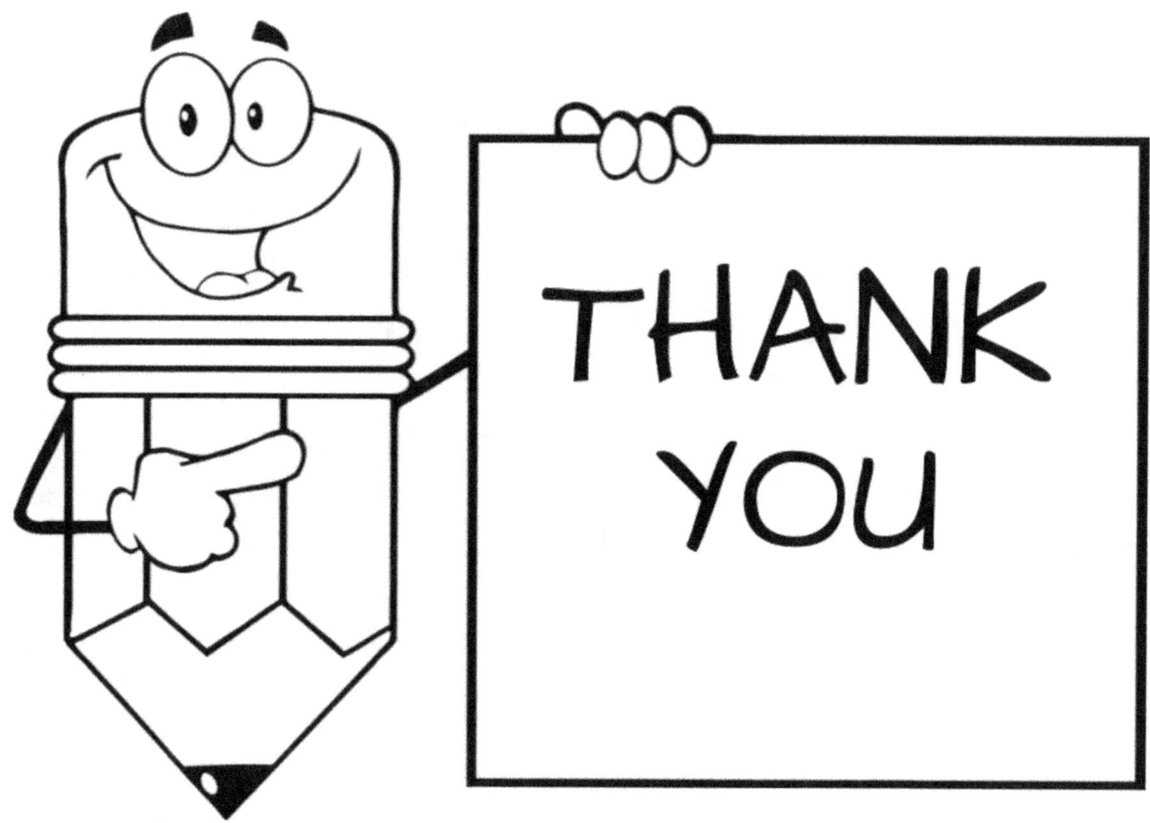